W9-CMM-315

TECHNICAL COLLEGE OF THE LOWCOUNTRY
LEARNING RESOURCES CENTER
POST OFFICE BOX 1288
BEAUFORT, SOUTH CAROLINA 29901-1288

UNDERSTANDING
PHILIP ROTH

Understanding Contemporary American Literature

Matthew J. Bruccoli, *Editor*

Understanding Bernard Malamud
by Jeffrey Helterman
Understanding James Dickey
by Ronald Baughman
Understanding John Hawkes
by Donald J. Greiner
Understanding Thomas Pynchon
by Robert D. Newman
Understanding Randall Jarrell
by J. A. Bryant, Jr.
Understanding Edward Albee
by Matthew C. Roudané
Understanding Contemporary American Drama
by William Herman
Understanding Vladimir Nabokov
by Stephen Jan Parker
Understanding Joyce Carol Oates
by Greg Johnson
Understanding Theodore Roethke
by Walter B. Kalaidjian
Understanding Mary Lee Settle
by George Garrett
Understanding Isaac Bashevis Singer
by Lawrence S. Friedman
Understanding George Garrett
by R. H. W. Dillard

Understanding Walker Percy
by Linda Whitney Hobson
Understanding Chicano Literature
by Carl R. Shirley and
Paula W. Shirley
Understanding Denise Levertov
by Harry Marten
Understanding Raymond Carver
by Arthur M. Saltzman
Understanding Katherine Anne Porter
by Darlene Harbour Unrue
Understanding Robert Bly
by William V. Davis
Understanding William Stafford
by Judith Kitchen
Understanding Carson McCullers
by Virginia Spencer Carr
Understanding John Barth
by Stan Fogel and
Gordon Slethaug
Understanding Ursula K. Le Guin
by Elizabeth Cummins
Understanding Contemporary American Science Fiction
by Thomas Clareson

UNDERSTANDING
Philip
ROTH

by MURRAY BAUMGARTEN
and BARBARA GOTTFRIED

TECHNICAL COLLEGE OF THE LOWCOUNTRY
LEARNING RESOURCES CENTER
POST OFFICE BOX 1288
BEAUFORT, SOUTH CAROLINA 29901-1288

UNIVERSITY OF SOUTH CAROLINA PRESS

TECHNICAL COLLEGE OF THE LOWCOUNTRY
LEARNING RESOURCES CENTER
POST OFFICE BOX 1288
BEAUFORT, SOUTH CAROLINA 29901-1288

Copyright © University of South Carolina 1990

Published in Columbia, South Carolina, by the
University of South Carolina Press

Manufactured in the United States of America

The following are reprinted by permission of Farrar, Straus and
Giroux, Inc.

Excerpts from *The Anatomy Lesson* by Philip Roth. Copyright © 1983
by Philip Roth.

Excerpts from *The Counterlife* by Philip Roth. Copyright © 1987 by
Philip Roth.

Excerpts from *The Facts* by Philip Roth. Copyright © 1988 by Philip
Roth.

Excerpts from *The Ghost Writer* by Philip Roth. Copyright © 1979
by Philip Roth.

Excerpts from *The Professor of Desire* by Philip Roth. Copyright ©
1977 by Philip Roth.

Excerpts from "The Prague Orgy" from *Zuckerman Bound* by Philip
Roth. Copyright © 1985 by Philip Roth.

Excerpts from *Zuckerman Unbound* by Philip Roth. Copyright © 1981
by Philip Roth.

Excerpts from *Portnoy's Complaint* by Philip Roth, copyright 1969 by
Philip Roth, are reprinted by permission of Random House.

Library of Congress Cataloging-in-Publication Data

Baumgarten, Murray.
   Understanding Philip Roth / by Murray Baumgarten and
Barbara Gottfried.
      p. cm. — (Understanding contemporary American literature)
   Includes bibliographical references.
   ISBN 0–87249–685–6
   1. Roth, Philip—Criticism and interpretation. I. Gottfried.
Barbara. II. Title. III. Series.
PS3568.0855Z57   1990
813'.54—dc20   89–49220
                                                           CIP

CONTENTS

Editor's Preface   vii

Acknowledgments   ix

Chapter 1   Understanding Philip Roth   1

Chapter 2   The Suburbs of Forgetfulness:
Goodbye, Columbus (1959)   21

Chapter 3   American Innocence/American
Anger: *Letting Go* (1962); *When She
Was Good* (1967)   60

Chapter 4   What DO Men Want, Dr. Roth?
or *Portnoy's Complaint* (1969)   77

Chapter 5   American Rites: *Our Gang* (1971); *The
Breast* (1972); *The Great American
Novel* (1973)   103

Chapter 6   Virtuoso Performances: *My Life as a
Man* (1974); *The Professor of Desire*
(1975)   132

Chapter 7   Boundaries: *The Ghost Writer* (1979);
Zuckerman Unbound (1981); *The
Anatomy Lesson* (1983)   155

Chapter 8   Counterlives:
The Counterlife (1987)   202

Chapter 9   Editing Himself and Others:
Criticism and
Autobiography   233

Bibliography   257

Index   267

EDITOR'S PREFACE

Understanding Contemporary American Literature has been planned as a series of guides or companions for students as well as good nonacademic readers. The editor and publisher perceive a need for these volumes because much of the influential contemporary literature makes special demands. Uninitiated readers encounter difficulty in approaching works that depart from the traditional forms and techniques of prose and poetry. Literature relies on conventions, but the conventions keep evolving; new writers form their own conventions—which in time may become familiar. Put simply, *UCAL* provides instruction in how to read certain contemporary writers—identifying and explicating their material, themes, use of language, point of view, structures, symbolism, and responses to experience.

The word *understanding* in the series title was deliberately chosen. Many willing readers lack an adequate understanding of how contemporary literature works; that is, what the author is attempting to express and the means by which it is conveyed. Although the criticism and analysis in the series have been aimed at a level of general accessibility, these introductory volumes are meant to be applied in conjunction with the works they cover. Thus they do not provide a substitute for the works and authors they introduce, but rather prepare the reader for more profitable literary experiences.

M. J. B

ACKNOWLEDGMENTS

Many colleagues have helped us in the course of our work. The advice and encouragement of the late Joseph Silverman was invaluable, as was that of Charles Neider, and Matthew Bruccoli. Margaret N. Gordon, Deborah Murphy, Judith Steen, and the other reference librarians of the University of California, Santa Cruz, McHenry Library, provided essential bibliographical assistance; they were seconded by Noah Kaplan, Mark Engel, Marc Moskowitz, and Erik Trump, who found the answers to innumerable queries. Our thanks go to John Jordan, Charles Smith, Deborah Gordon, and Sheila Baumgarten for their thoughtful counsel, and to the Committee on Research of the Academic Senate, University of California, Santa Cruz, and the Research Relations Fund of the University of Hawaii at Manoa for their financial support.

UNDERSTANDING
PHILIP ROTH

CHAPTER ONE

Understanding
Philip Roth

Career

Philip Roth was born in Newark, New Jersey, on 19 March 1933 to Herman and Bess Finkel Roth. In his autobiography Roth notes that his father, after several low-paying jobs and the bankruptcy of a family shoe store, felt fortunate to have gotten a job as an insurance salesman for Metropolitan Life in the era of narrowing boundaries and limited possibilities ushered in by the Depression. He was one of the very few Jews hired by the corporation. Like most of his generation he "worked a six-day week, evenings included," and was grateful for the steady, if modest, living the insurance work provided. His mother, Roth recalls, nurtured him, running an orderly and calm household amid the patriotic fervor occasioned by World War II. The graphic evidence of the Holocaust, featured in newsreels and stark photographs in magazines and newspapers, reinforced the Roth family's pride in their American haven. Later, the Cold War and its propaganda mills made Roth aware of how vulnerable he and his contemporaries had become to the rhetoric of an ideological patriotism.

From 1946 to 1950 Roth attended Weequahic High School, played baseball, clowned with his friends, read avidly in the Newark Public Library, and discovered the diverse neighborhoods of his city, then an intense if less sophisticated outpost of European immigrant culture than New York City, its enormous counterpart across the Hudson. In 1950 he enrolled at Newark College of Rutgers University, but in 1951 he transferred to Bucknell University in Pennsylvania to escape the "provincialism" of Newark and discover the "rest of America."[1]

At Bucknell he published his first story, "Philosophy," in the literary magazine, *Et Cetera*, which he helped to establish and edit. He graduated magna cum laude and Phi Beta Kappa with a BA in English in 1954. In 1955 he received his MA in English from the University of Chicago. That same year he entered the army, but due to a back injury he suffered during basic training he was quickly discharged. He returned to study for the PhD in English at the University of Chicago, but dropped out of the program in 1957. By this time he had published four stories in literary magazines, two of which won awards and were reprinted. With the help of grants from the National Institute of Arts and Letters, the Houghton Mifflin Literary Fellowship, and a Guggenheim Fellowship, he began work on a collection of stories. In 1959, just as *Goodbye, Columbus* was about to be published, he married Margaret Martinson Williams.

CAREER OVERVIEW

The marriage proved disastrous, and they separated three years later.

In 1960 Roth began teaching in the Writers' Workshop at the University of Iowa, and two years later became writer-in-residence at Princeton University. During this time Roth wrote his first full-length novel, *Letting Go* (1962), and began work on *When She Was Good* (1967). Though both were satiric, neither was humorous; both novels focused on frustration and suppressed rage,and received only lukewarm critical praise. In both novels the protagonists attempt to rebel against the limitations of their time and place. Their rebellion fails because they are isolated and directionless, without effective means to channel their dissatisfactions. There are comic moments in each novel, but their overall effect is of unrelieved, grim, and hopeless lives. In the early works Roth's "young man," like Stephen Dedalus, Joyce's hero, comes of age in a time, place, and family he both hates and loves. The novels explore the negotiations and compromises of that youth, of love and of marriage, which are complicated by the protagonist's pursuit of an artistic vocation or an intellectual life. But unlike Joyce's Stephen Dedalus the censor is not so much the protagonist's parents, or even his environment, as it is the inner workings of his own psyche. At this time Roth began to publish excerpts from his novels in progress, a pattern he was to follow for many years. In 1968 his wife, from whom he had been separated for six years, was killed in an automobile accident. A year later, in 1969, Paramount released the film version of *Goodbye, Columbus*, just as *Portnoy's Complaint* was completed. That same year Roth was elected to the National Institute of Arts and Letters. In 1972 the film of *Portnoy* was released by Warner Brothers, coinciding with the publication of his ambiguous and troubling novella, *The Breast*.

Roth has been a controversial figure since he published his first collection of short stories and a novella, *Goodbye, Columbus*, in 1959. Critical response was overwhelmingly positive. The volume was hailed as fresh and original—a gritty, realistic departure from the cool, terse, arch, and artful stories of the reigning modernist writers Flaubert, Joyce, Hemingway, and Katherine Mansfield. In Roth, Leslie Fiedler noted, Newark had at last found its poet laureate—a writer as "vulgar, comical, subtle, pathetic and dirty" as the city itself.[2] *Goodbye, Columbus* won both the National Book Award and the Jewish Book Council's Daroff Award. But at the same time that Roth was praised by critics, he was condemned by Jewish community leaders as an anti-Semite who portrayed Jews as "depraved and lecherous." His work, they asserted, could only lead readers to conclude "that this country—nay that the world—would be a much better and happier place without Jews."[3] This pattern of praise for the literary qualities of his work, coupled with criticism of his complex portraits of Jews, has continued throughout Roth's career. All his fiction, published between 1959 and 1987, has received mixed

CAREER OVERVIEW

reviews. For every critic who has praised Roth's work, there has been one who has found his work lacking in depth or moral seriousness. Nevertheless, Roth's double-edged portraits of Jews, writers, and American family life have found a worldwide audience. Many have appreciated the deft balance of his satire, and he has become a popular and important writer both in the United States and abroad.

Roth's early novels and tales contain the potential for the comic explosiveness of his best-known novel, *Portnoy's Complaint*. Published in 1969 at the height of the political and racial unrest that led to the burning of whole sections of Roth's Newark and other American cities, strident student protests against the Vietnam war, and the beginning of the women's liberation movement in America, *Portnoy's* sexual explicitness and political rebellion capture the era's destruction of political and social boundaries, as well as its greater freedom and opening of new possibilities for both women and men. Echoing many of the themes of *Goodbye, Columbus*, *Portnoy's Complaint* balanced and completed Roth's study of the American family. In *Letting Go* Roth had explored the relationship of confused Jewish fathers and their perplexing, disappointing sons, while in *When She Was Good* he had focused on the obedient Christian daughter and her abusive, alcoholic father; now in *Portnoy*, Roth extended his analysis to the relationship of the Jewish son and his overbearing mother. What Roth was to call the "Bacchus of Hometown, U.S.A."

was now complemented by the "Cleopatra of the kitchen."[4]

After *Portnoy*, Roth turned to political satire. In keeping with the tenor of the early 1970s he published the sardonic "On the Air" (1970) in the *New American Review* and the savage *Our Gang* (1971). *The Great American Novel*, published in 1973, intertwines politics and baseball. A complex and self-conscious parody of American literary traditions, it is also an attack on the political legacy of McCarthyism and the deformation of the American dream of success during the era of Vietnam. In 1974 he continued his experiments with voice and narrative strategy, publishing *My Life as a Man*.

Convinced that American reality outdoes the imagination and inventiveness of American writers—a central theme of *Reading Myself and Others* (1975)—Roth from this point on in his career focuses on the career of the artist and the process of fiction-making. In his next novel, *The Professor of Desire*, published in 1977, the adventures of the protagonist, David Kepesh, a teacher of literature, illuminate the relationship between what one reads and what one is. Kepesh alternately embraces the intellectual, moral life, and an unsublimated life of desire and debauchery as he lives out the conflict suggested by the title of the novel. In the Zuckerman trilogy—*The Ghost Writer* (1979), *Zuckerman Unbound* (1981), and *The Anatomy Lesson* (1983)—as well as his latest novel in which Nathan Zuckerman continues to fulfill the hero's role, *The Counterlife* (1987), Roth carries forward his exploration of the fictions of self-consciousness and maps new regions of the game of fiction-making with which to tease his readers. These are among Roth's most sophisticated novels, and his most elegiac.

Despite the difficulties Jewish children and parents have in dealing with each other in his fiction, in real life Roth has been close to his parents, providing for them financially with the proceeds of his best-sellers and dedicating his most recent novel, *The Counterlife*, to his father on his eighty-fifth birthday, and his autobiography to his brother. Although he has not been a recluse like J. D. Salinger or Thomas Pynchon, Roth has guarded his privacy. Since 1970 he has taught occasionally at the University of Pennsylvania, serving as an adjunct professor of English, and most recently has been appointed to the faculty at Hunter College of the City University of New York. For more than a decade now Roth and the British actress Claire Bloom have been together, with Roth tending to divide his time between England and the United States.

Overview

Philip Roth's comic novels explore the moral complexities of modern experience. The enormous changes that have characterized recent decades form one of the recurring themes of his fictional world, as he analyzes the ways in which desire, art, and the moral imagination intertwine and together shape the ability of characters and social groups to deal with the tumultuous, cruel, and violent twentieth century. In its imaginative re-creation of the new possibilities offered Americans and Jews by modern culture, his writing engages and interrogates modern history. Creatures of blood and imagination, his protagonists must deal with a comic world of serious consequences. Much of Roth's work satirizes the obsessions and delusions of neurotics, yet his deft comic touch tempers the sharpness of the criticism. His characters inhabit a comic world always on the verge of spinning out of control. Nevertheless, the moral dimension of their choices is paramount. In Roth's satiric universe the comic moment reveals the underlying seriousness of contemporary life.

Roth's early satires focus on the complacency of second-generation suburban Jews, who on the one hand deny their cultural heritage and on the other consciously limit the range of their participation in American political life. They also explore the role and influence of the American artist/intellectual. Each tale grows out of a sharp perception of the necessity to assert the self, despite the pressure to conform, and make a responsible moral choice. Individuality and integrity are at stake, so parents and inherited loyalties must be confronted, renewed, or sometimes sacrificed. Roth gives these traditional literary themes of the novel of education—the *Bildungsroman*—a special flavor by locat-

CAREER OVERVIEW

ing them in the lives of lower-middle-class Jews of Newark and New York City as they embark on the American adventure of upward social mobility and suburbanization. The historical context is always clear, and the traumatic events of Western culture since World War II press insistently upon Roth's characters. The great Depression of the 1930s, World War II, the Holocaust, the Cold War, McCarthyism, the Vietnam war, the protests and demonstrations of the 1960s and 1970s, and the women's movement form the boundaries of their worlds. Roth's eye for telling comic detail and his brilliant ear for the varieties of American speech, as well as the vivid and gritty sources of his characters, make his work original, sociologically accurate, and controversial.

The Jewish tales, most notably *Goodbye, Columbus* and *Portnoy's Complaint*, do not center on traditional Jewish holidays but on weekend adventures, weekday work experiences, and hurried, reluctant encounters with older relatives over elaborate meals. Immigrant values of not wasting something as precious as food become the obsessive remnants of a neglected religious tradition. As well, the fashionable American clothing of these characters—elegant suits and Brooks Brothers shirts, tuxedos, tennis outfits—reveal what has changed in their lives. Arrayed in these outfits, these characters have joined the American world of individual choice, where shopping in the great supermarket of endless possibility is the only option. The intimacies of religious communal life—of the *communion* of bed and board, of sacredness created out of the mundane everyday world—have been forgotten. The public world of traditional Jewish life in which the values of the community are enacted in public and publicly scrutinized—what Eli Peck in "Eli, the Fanatic" embodies in donning identifiable Jewish clothing at highly charged moments—has been replaced by private sexual encounters like Neil and Brenda's in "Goodbye, Columbus." Such very modern relationships do not lead to family ties and communal consequences; instead, they remain personal adventures. And in this contrasting of the fuller possibilities of public life with the realities of suburban conformism, Roth reveals the hidden poverty of spirit beneath the surface opulence of 1950s individualism, and delineates his satiric values much as the sociologist David Riesman, also a University of Chicago man, had done a decade earlier in *The Lonely Crowd.* What the suburbs have are the sexual secrets of Epstein and the political conspiracies of Tricky E. Dixon, glimpsed like film images in the dark. What they lack is the fullness of communal life suggested in "Goodbye, Columbus" by Aunt Gladys and Uncle Max.

Roth is a writer who focuses on contradictions. His world is filled with a surplus of meanings; excess abounds, and things turn into their opposites. A novelist of ideas, he dramatizes the process of thinking about this dynamic world. Whatever the setting, the place in which the action occurs is also one that includes the history of parallel events explored in the classics of Western literature. Thus Prague is full of meaning for David Kepesh in *The Professor of Desire* precisely because it is Kafka's city—the Prague of Gregor Samsa in "The Metamorphosis" and of Kafka's own familial and personal tragedy, as well as the site of the Soviet stifling of Czech liberty since the invasion of 1968. As an American satirist Roth shares many of the liberal social, political, and cultural concerns of other contemporary novelists. He was among the first American writers to bring into his fiction an awareness of how the murder of six million Jews by the Nazis has shaped the modern world. Roth also shares with his Eastern European colleagues, Milan Kundera and Josef Skvorecky, a sense, evident in their art, of the links between the obsessive eroticism of modern life and its totalitarian political dilemmas.

The central ideal of American culture Roth confronts and subverts in his work is that of character. There are few heroes in his fiction; most of his protagonists have the obverse qualities of the all-American boy or girl. Characters in all of Roth's tales suffer from unnamed afflictions against which they struggle. Their desperation grows as they find themselves, despite strenuous efforts, unable to channel their dissatisfaction and change their situations. Yet when they embrace their suffering as their destiny, they only make their predicament worse. Though excess is their condition, sainthood and martyrdom are not available in Roth's comic universe.

In Roth's work individual events become representative of the experiences of the group, for his subject is not one character's life but the life experiences of a generation. Roth's personal knowledge of the American army after World War II informs many of his tales; yet it would be a mistake to take any of them as autobiographical statements. Rather, his work is part of an American tradition of "fictionalized recall"; that is, Roth does not, despite what some readers believe, write autobiographical novels, though he draws upon personal knowledge which he transforms into fiction.[5] The resulting characters stand for a generation's experience and do not function individually as role models. The moral accounting of character central to the great realistic writers is transformed by Roth into the process of charting the relationships of a minority and its enveloping majority culture. Roth is aware that ethnicity depends upon politics for its definition, for what defines a given ethnic group is the result of implicit and sometimes explicit negotiation with the majority. This realization of the interdependence of politics and ethnicity allows him to map the history of a characteristic American group. Roth's characters do not embody the ethos of individualism; rather, the status of the individual is the central problem in his work. Focusing on individual figures, he writes about them as particular and specific embodiments of the general experience of a characteristic American group.

This group is most clearly designated in the Yiddish/German roots of many characters' names, which often reveal by an ironic twist the condition from which they suffer. Paul *Herz* is despite his name not all heart; Neil *Klugman* is smart enough to be cynical yet not smart enough to keep from sexual entanglement; Nathan *Zuckerman*, entranced by literature, is, in one of the ironic possibilities always present in Yiddish, not sweet and winsome despite the sugar his name refers to; Dr. *Spielvogel* is a bird at play; and Jimmy *Lustig* lusts and glitters. Roth makes the reader pay attention as well to the political implications of names like Nathan Marx and Roland Agni, whose name echoes both the lamb of God and Spiro Agnew, the disgraced vice-president of Nixon's first term in office, and Sheldon Grossbart, who is gross in his wheedling. The sounds of their names add meanings: Dr. Klinger rings a bell; Claire Ovington is clear-sighted and nurturing; David Kepesh is the beloved son, as his first name suggests, while his last name perhaps echoes the Yiddish word for head, smart, an intellectual. Helen Baird, whose beauty like Helen of Troy's is destructive, reveals/bares all, and Mordecai Lippman gives everyone lots of lip.

What the reader knows about the names of their conditions these characters cannot. Alexander Portnoy, whose last name is Russian for tailor, gives his name to a psychological complex while dramatizing the effort to explore it by his complaint. Like Nathan Zuckerman and David Kepesh, he becomes obsessed with his affliction in order, as he explains in his monologue, to escape from it. The reader, however, knows that he is making things worse. Roth deploys a canny psychoanalytically oriented psychology that calls attention to the obsessive orality of his characters—or, by contrast, to their insistent silence. Trying to discover who they are, most of them talk too much. Libby Herz and Lucy Nelson cannot rid themselves of their insistent, scheming inner voices. Neither can Gabe Wallach's father, Alexander Portnoy, or Alvin Pepler shut up. It takes a broken jaw to silence Nathan Zuckerman. In their own ways each of these characters is an immigrant, whose verbal display in the language of the new land is an obsessive effort to gain acceptance. The right performance will prove he or she is indeed an American; their excess reveals the desperation of the excluded and the marginal.

Roth chooses the occupations of his characters carefully. Like David Kepesh in *The Professor of Desire*, they are what they *profess*, in the original meaning of the word, and thus reveal the values by which they live. Neil works in the Newark Public Library because he believes the accumulated wisdom of Western culture will make him a better person. David Kepesh is a teacher of literature because he believes books contain the secrets of desire. However, everyday life is full of surprises that test a character's values, and when Neil falls in love with Brenda, he has to rethink his priorities. Lucy Nelson does not want to marry Roy Bassart, but her pregnancy and the doctor's refusal to let her terminate it make her agree to become his wife. Possessions and money are less important to Roth's characters than moral relationships with other people. Even when Theresa agrees to sell her baby to Gabe in *Letting Go*, her decision emerges from a moral calculation.

Though character types recur in Roth's work, each character has a slightly different perspective which distinguishes him. Gabe Wallach in *Letting Go* resembles Neil Klugman of "Goodbye, Columbus"; however, Gabe is a more educated person than Neil and has financial advantages that Neil does not. As a result Gabe is not overwhelmed by suburban affluence but instead falls in love with the hard-working lower-middle-class Martha Regenhart. Often an outsider, the main character must chart his way to the center of the social situation. In most cases the males seek to conquer through the exercise of sexual and intellectual prowess. The upper-middle-class women are not tricked into permanent relationships by sexual pleasure, which they accept without ambivalence, as does Birgitta in *The Professor of Desire;* the lower-middle-class women are willing to exchange sexual favors for upward social mobility, as Maureen does in *My Life as a Man*. Yet neither class nor institutional connections fully determine a character's view. Each is presented as a blend of insider and outsider, two complicated parents, varied institutional links, and cultural views. The historical moment also offers as well as closes off possibilities. For this reason Peter Tarnopol discusses the nature of marriage in the 1950s, while Alexander Portnoy is obsessed by polio, Joe DiMaggio, and the Holocaust. What is determining is the attitude each character has toward her or his gender identity and that of the opposite sex.

Despite the presence of male narrators, women are central to Roth's work. The ways in which they affect the main character are presented ironically, for the males rarely see more than they desire. Their interactions reveal what these characters are about; Peter Tarnopol does not know much about Maureen Walker when he first meets her; Nathan Zuckerman is not sure why he rejects Sharon Shatsky for Lydia; David Kepesh cannot comprehend why he left Dina Dornbusch for Helen Baird; the meaning of their choices reflects upon their personal desires. The plots of these stories of education lead to discovery of the grounds of incompatibility. Though everyone must choose, the conditions of choice are blindness *and* insight, seeing and the impossibility of seeing, and the result is always fateful. There are few happy relationships in Roth's work; rather, he charts the different ways in which men and women can make each other miserable, as a way of understanding their partial and limited view of human life.

As a satirist Roth depends upon stereotypic characterization. The accuracy of his portraits draws the reader into the fictional process and encourages him to complete the sketches, at the same time that they mock the reader for accepting their validity. The deft and vivid description of the social surface of everyday life brings class, gender, and ethnicity into play. Most of Roth's middle-class male Jewish protagonists are narcissists; his often lower-class Gentile heroines are abused and battered. Roth plots a collision course for these conventional figures from different realms, for in this universe opposites attract, as both encounter the social and political barriers that confine them. The satire moves from visual presentation and the accurate rendering of dialogue into the exploration of psychology and self-consciousness, thereby deepening stereotypes into original and living characters.

None of the writers with whom Roth is most often compared—Saul Bellow, Bernard Malamud, Mordecai Richler—evoke the surfaces of everyday life with his vivid visual fullness. Furthermore, Roth's work consistently depicts a more realistic social experience than theirs, even as he deploys more prominently than they do a complex psychology of familial motivation and immigrant hope in his work. Nevertheless, Roth's prose is not dominated by the overt Yiddishisms of Malamud and Richler or the cerebral aggression of Bellow's Jewish intellectuals. While Yiddish, the language of the immigrants, and the brilliant intellectual aggressiveness of the new generation of Jewish professionals play a significant part in his work, the linguistic quickness and agility of urban life is its primary quality, mirroring the nimbleness with which his characters move through the dynamic American suburb and cityscape. Writing in a supple, vivid American English, Roth stakes out a new area for Jewish writing. He defines the shape of a Jewish literature—that is, writing which charts the fateful experiences of the Jews—in a non-Jewish language accessible to all Americans. In their desperate quest for selfhood his Jewish characters echo the experiences of the classic American heroes, from Ishmael in Melville's *Moby-Dick*, to Huckleberry Finn and Jay Gatsby. The communal conditions of Roth's satiric art define the function of this new American literature: in exploring the Jewish experience of the suburbs that began in the 1950s, it articulates the importance of American memory.

As they embark on their voyage of self-discovery, Roth's heroes and heroines alike discover reservoirs of cultural and personal self-hatred. Their dynamic universe, however, does not stop for answers or resolutions, so these characters respond by renewing their quests and their questionings. Similarly, the literary masters so often cited in his work—Rilke, Kafka, Chekhov, Babel, Dickens, Shakespeare, and Swift—are all notable for the fluidity and change of their worlds and the power of their questioning of the accepted social order. Though not often directly named in Roth's work but frequently alluded to, biblical Job, who keeps on asking fundamental questions about the nature of the universe though constantly cautioned by his "comforters" to be still, is an informing force throughout. And the bemused satisfaction Job attains at the outcome of his story, when he is rewarded for his faithful questioning with a double portion of all he had previously lost, resonates in the ironic endings of Roth's tales, as if the Book of Job were rewritten for the Marx brothers.

Two other figures have helped to shape Roth's literary work. He acknowledges the impact of Lionel Trilling's analysis of the relationship of manners, morals, and the modern novel. Roth also draws on Trilling's exploration of the connections between literature and politics in "The Liberal Imagination." The other influence is that of Cervantes, who transformed the picaresque tale and the pastoral romance, with its interpolated tales, into the profound comic satire of *Don Quixote*. Roth's fusing of the farcical and the picaresque echoes Cervantes; so too does Roth's use of the comic to reveal moral complexity. And he follows Cervantes's lead in bringing together dramatic and realistic modes to create a perspectival realm in which the comic imagination reigns supreme.

Notes

1. *The Facts: A Novelist's Autobiography* (New York: Farrar, Straus, 1988); excerpted in *The New York Times Book Review* 18 Oct. 1987.

2. Leslie Fiedler, "The Image of Newark and the Indignities of Love: Notes on Philip Roth," *Critical Essays on Philip Roth*, ed. Sanford Pinsker (Boston: Hall, 1982) 24.

3. Dan Isaac, "In Defense of Philip Roth," Pinsker 182.

4. Roth, *Reading Myself and Others* (New York: Farrar, Straus, 1975) 66.

5. See Tony Tanner, *City of Words: American Fiction 1950–1970* (New York: Harper, 1971), ch. 13, "Fictionalized Recall."

CHAPTER TWO

The Suburbs of Forgetfulness: *Goodbye, Columbus* (1959)

"Goodbye, Columbus"

The Jewish immigrant past and American present, city and suburb, lower-middle and upper-middle class collide in this comic satire. "Goodbye, Columbus" encompasses the conflicts between two generations and two different ways of life. Its narrator, Neil Klugman, is a lower-middle-class Newark boy; Brenda, the girl he loves, is from Short Hills, an elegant suburb; they meet at the country-club swimming pool. Their encounter is the result of a mutual sexual attraction rather than the shared interest of communal life, family connections, or political action. Neil and Brenda define their relationship not in terms of classic Jewish values of family and religious tradition but the chivalric myth of knight and lady.

In its emphasis on seeing, "Goodbye, Columbus" has much of the visual impact of a film. Neil as narrator describes what happens as if he were a camera eye and the unfolding experiences in which he participates were

21

a romantic movie of a summer's love affair. He presents himself as detached and disinterested, but what he registers is more complicated than he is willing to admit. "The first time I saw Brenda she asked me to hold her glasses. Then she stepped out to the edge of the diving board and looked foggily into the pool; it could have been drained, myopic Brenda would never have known it." Not only does Brenda as an object of desire for Neil come into focus at the beginning of the tale, so too do Neil's complicated feelings for her, of which he is not fully aware. As the novel begins, Neil quite literally sees what Brenda cannot, and he translates this visual acuity into a presumed moral advantage. While he is indeed a sharp-eyed critic of what Brenda is up to, he does not fully acknowledge what is happening to him. "She dove beautifully, and a moment later she was swimming back to the side of the pool, her head of short-clipped auburn hair held up, straight ahead of her, as though it were a rose on a long stem." Comparing Brenda's head to "a rose on a long stem" makes her into a figure of potential romance. The sentence also suggests that Brenda self-consciously presents herself to the narrator; she is performing for him. Roth's prose makes it clear that Neil is an open-eyed participant in his own seduction.

The response Brenda seeks from Neil takes the rest of the paragraph to emerge. Once more it comes through as a fully realized filmic sequence.

THE SUBURBS OF FORGETFULNESS

She glided to the edge and then was beside me. "Thank you," she said, her eyes watery though not from the water. She extended a hand for her glasses but did not put them on until she turned and headed away. I watched her move off. Her hands suddenly appeared behind her. She caught the bottom of her suit between thumb and index finger and flicked what flesh had been showing back where it belonged. My blood jumped.[1]

This exclamation of aroused desire punctuates the vivid opening paragraph, revealing that the young man from Newark who has posed as a wry and somewhat detached, amused, and even cynical observer is no longer merely a spectator. "That night, before dinner, I called her." Neil Klugman, whose name ironically means "smart," in Yiddish, has not been able to resist temptation, and plunges into a summer romance.

In this encounter Roth captures the Jewish moment of suburbanization of American life. Brenda and Neil are not only the quintessential American girl and boy but as well a phenomenon of the 1950s, when the democratic possibilities of upward social mobility were coming true for large segments of the American population which had, up until then, been on the margins of American life. Sharing in the new prosperity, Brenda's family lives in newly elegant Short Hills, while her father commutes to the center of Newark where his plumbing-supply business is located. Neil, however, lives in Newark with his Aunt Gladys and Uncle Max, since his parents have left the humid East Coast climate for Arizona because of their chronic asthma. Working downtown in the Newark Public Library, he does not share in the advantages of an increasingly prosperous American middle-class population that, after World War II, had been moving in ever-increasing numbers from the growing racial, cultural, and ethnic diversity of the American city to the developing suburbs. Neil's meeting with Brenda is his first taste of affluence.

In "Goodbye, Columbus" the differences between city and suburb are translated into attitudes toward sexuality. Neil seeks to discover whether there is a necessary connection between Brenda's sexual openness to him and her family's wealth, which he alternately prizes and scorns. Neil is unsure whether he seeks Brenda's social position and money, sexual initiation, or her love. His ambivalence leads him to accept with startling passivity the various tasks she expects him to perform, including holding her glasses while she swims, waiting for her to finish her tennis game, or taking care of her kid sister, Julie. His words, however, consistently have an irritated, angry edge. Brenda imposes tasks on Neil as if their lives were a chivalric drama of knight and princess, but at the same time she appears to be readily paying him for his services (and leading him on to new challenges) with sexual favors. Neil cannot decide whether Brenda is testing him to find out if he might be a worthwhile partner for her and, despite his lower-middle-class origins and educa-

THE SUBURBS OF FORGETFULNESS

tion, is sufficiently malleable to meet her needs, or whether he is simply her summer adventure. Neil's keen city vision and abrasive, aggressive behavior defend him against an acknowledgment of how much he is in love with Brenda and her affluent world.

In this novella Jewish and American history intersect in the two contradictory worlds that come to a focus in the encounter of Brenda and Neil. Neil's city toughness is mirrored in his Aunt Gladys and Uncle Max's matter-of-factness, their tight living quarters, and their understanding that the only way to get ahead is to work very hard. Brenda's summer world is one of endless sport—of swimming, tennis, ping-pong—in which these games become the model for all human activities. Functions are reversed: the Patimkin refrigerator is a horn of plenty, while the trees in the garden literally bear the fruit of sports equipment, as if those expensive toys which are the sign of suburban leisure were a natural part of the Patimkin environment. Brenda's suburban country-club life style is utterly separate from her father's world of dirty, physically taxing work. His prosperous business is still in Newark, the gritty city the Patimkin family left behind in moving to the suburban Garden of Eden of Short Hills.

Though he is fascinated by its abundance and the fullness of possibilities Short Hills offers, Neil also sees its disguises. His skeptical, somewhat distanced perspective reveals the price of entry into the country-club world. Brenda's bobbed nose, surgically altered to make it prettier as well as to make her less obviously Jewish, is but one part of the cost of admission. The growing inability of parents and children to communicate is another. Neil's values, so much closer to the immigrant world committed to work and achievement, make him someone that at one point in the story Mr. Patimkin can respect—by contrast with his feelings for his own son, Ron, who does not share these values. Unlike the lower-middle-class world of Newark with its hard though satisfying physical labor, and the honest, if underpaid, public services of library and state university, the upper-class-world of Short Hills cordons off work and keeps it out of sight; nothing costs too much, and only the right appearance and good looks matter. Suburban men and women are handsome, beautiful, and a homogeneous lot. Like Ron and Brenda they go away to colleges which seal their Americanness. Urban folk, by contrast, come in all sorts of sizes and colors, and have names like Klugman and Patimkin that are the orthographical equivalents of their heterogeneous shapes. They have warts and bumps on their noses, and like Neil they go to school in their ethnically and racially diverse neighborhoods.

The summer heat of Newark relents a little in the evening. Aunt Gladys and Uncle Max sit outside and enjoy the breeze. A vaguely dissatisfied Neil finds their small pleasures frustrating. Aunt Gladys's explanations of why she does things her way irritate him. To expose their distance from each other Roth has his characters

THE SUBURBS OF FORGETFULNESS

speak out of their own terms of reference to characters who no longer share those values and ways. The result is a comedy of misapprehension, as, for example, when Neil suggests to Aunt Gladys that "tonight we all eat together. It's hot, it'll be easier for you." But Aunt Gladys sticks to her own ways. "Sure, I should serve four different meals at once. You eat pot roast, Susan with the cottage cheese, Max has steak. Friday night is his steak night, I wouldn't deny him. And I'm having a little cold chicken. I should jump up and down twenty different times? What am I, a workhorse?" Neil's response—"Why don't we all have steak, or cold chicken"—sounds reasonable, but that is not how Aunt Gladys takes it: "Twenty years I'm running a house. Go call your girl friend" (4–5). Neil is particularly adept at spotting the contradictions in Aunt Gladys's hard-working lower-middle-class life style; nevertheless, this does not make it easier for him to deal with the contradictions in his own life. Though he is scornful of the affluence of the suburbs, Neil wants more than the stifling city can offer him. His ambivalence is resolved temporarily when he interprets Brenda's invitation to visit Short Hills as a promise to stay and taste its pastoral delights.

The plot of the comedy at first mirrors Neil's desire, as boy-meets-girl and then boy-gets-girl, coming to an ironic conclusion with the boy-loses-girl episode that fulfills the romance pattern. Along the way Roth defers the action by interspersing scenes that reveal Neil's divided loyalties. Neil's job in the library is posed against Brenda's country-club afternoons. Her sister, Julie, an obviously spoiled child, is contrasted to a young black schoolboy, with whom Neil identifies, who comes to the library every day to look at the sensual pictures of Gauguin. Neil watches out for him and reserves the books the boy particularly wants even when others ask for them. But he treats Brenda's sister with contempt, taking out on her his frustrations at not having the advantages of the Patimkins.

Even the sexual encounters with Brenda turn out to be unexpectedly frustrating for Neil. He discovers that what their bodies can manage they cannot express more fully. Neil is forced to consider the possibility that except for the fact of their mutual sexual attraction he and Brenda actually have little in common. They do not know how to talk about the meaning of their relationship and build it into a shared world. Their mutual and reciprocal incomprehensibility is most clearly expressed in the childishness of their dialogue, when, for instance, Brenda turns to Neil on what amounts to their first date and asks, "If I let you kiss me would you stop being nasty?" The sexual favors Neil seeks with the intensity of an ambitious working-class boy Brenda bestows with the ease and abandon of the upper-class girl.

We had to take about two too many steps to keep the approach from being awkward, but we pursued the impulse and kissed. I felt her hand on the back of my neck

THE SUBURBS OF FORGETFULNESS

and so I tugged her towards me, too violently perhaps, and slid my own hands across the side of her body and around to her back. I felt the wet spots on her shoulder blades, and beneath them, I'm sure of it, a faint flutter- ing, as though something stirred so deep in her breasts, so far back it could make itself felt through her shirt. It was like the fluttering of wings, tiny wings no bigger than her breasts. The smallness of the wings did not bother me—it would not take an eagle to carry me up those lousy hundred and eighty feet that make summer nights so much cooler in Short Hills than they are in Newark (14).

Neil's resentment at the advantages of wealth and status, which he does not share with her, drives him toward Brenda at the same time that it blinds him to the causes of their attraction to each other. "Do you love me, Neil?" Brenda asks one night when they are swim- ming alone at the country club. "I did not answer," Neil says. "I'll sleep with you whether you do nor not, so tell me the truth," Brenda continues her inquiry. " 'That was pretty crude.' 'Don't be prissy,' she said. 'No, I mean a crude thing to say about me.' 'I don't under- stand,' she said, and she didn't" (51). Both are confused as to whether they love or merely lust for each other.

For Brenda and Neil sexual intimacy is easy and difficult at the same time. They discover they can make love in the room where Neil stays over, almost when- ever they want to. Unlike the cramped Klugman apart- ment in Newark where Neil has to lock himself in the

closet to phone Brenda and talk to her with some sem-
blance of privacy, the Patimkin house is so large that
everyone has a room of her or his own. Privacy is paramount, and everyone is left alone to do what he or she
wants to. Nevertheless, Brenda and Neil have a vexed
relationship which they carry forward by negotiating
the management of their sexual contacts, displacing the
possibility of real intimacy into the details of their encounters. Often they sound more like experienced lovers managing an affair than young lovers experiencing
the fullness of sexual intimacy for the first time. As
Brenda and Neil perform sexually for each other, the
social, economic, and psychological differences at the
root of their inability to communicate begin to make
their presence felt. Masked by their emphasis on sexuality, these difficulties cannot fully be dealt with, and
break their relationship apart. "Goodbye, Columbus"
repeats the pattern of hopeful encounter and failed relationship of *The Great Gatsby*; like Gatsby, Neil wants
desperate romance to blossom into marriage. But despite the link of their common Jewish heritage, the gaps
of class and moral consciousness between Neil and
Brenda are too great for their relationship to succeed.
What Brenda's brother, Ron, manages to do in marrying
Harriet, Neil and Brenda cannot achieve.

As he reluctantly takes care of Julie one evening
while the family is driving Ron to the airport, Neil wan-
ders through the spacious Patimkin home and discovers
the previously unimagined possibilities of suburban

THE SUBURBS OF FORGETFULNESS

life. There are separate bedrooms for all the children; there is a room dedicated to television-watching. Functions that are jumbled together in his aunt and uncle's apartment are honored with their own rooms: for the Patimkins privacy and gracious living go together. The size of the suburban house and its specialization of functions by room make it possible to hide the past, once so integral and jumbled together. Neil discovers that the finished basement—the heart of the suburban ideal—includes a wet bar. In the "bacchanalian paraphernalia" with which it is equipped—"plentiful, orderly, and untouched, as it can be only in the bar of a wealthy man who never entertains drinking people, who himself does not drink, who, in fact, gets a fishy look from his wife when every several months he takes a shot of schnapps before dinner" (41–42)—Neil discovers the ambivalence of this newly rich family. The Patimkins are caught between the demands of their Newark Jewish ethnicity and the desire to show that they have arrived in Short Hills by emulating the ways of its Protestant upper class; their ambivalence echoes the complexity of his own desires. But just as there is no spatial integration of different functions in this suburban house, so there is no spiritual, economic, or communal hierarchy of values. The Patimkins are held together as a family by a system of programmed responses to conspicuous consumption, including food, rather than the values of the close-knit family of the urban Jewish neighborhood.

Brenda's brother, Ron, has no interest in the family business or work ethic. For him the fraternity and collegiate sports are paramount, replacing immediate and local family and neighborhood ties with the abstract and removed loyalties of alma mater. The title of the novella is taken from Ron's fraternity song, "Goodbye, Columbus." The phrase refers to the city of Columbus, Ohio, where Ohio State, the university he has attended, is located, but also ironically evokes the world of the Jewish immigrant by pointing to the discoverer of the New World, Christopher Columbus, and bidding him goodbye. In its focus on sports and college life the "Goodbye, Columbus" song reveals that Ron has substituted the masculine ideals of assimilated American life for traditional Jewish values. The same shallow values color the entire experience of Brenda's family and reveal the superficiality their new wealth has brought. Seeing the process of suburbanization through Neil's eyes, hearing the "Goodbye, Columbus" song through Neil's ears, makes the judgment of their inadequacies possible. The fact that Neil, the city kid, wants Brenda, the suburban girl, further reveals the ways in which the ideal of urban life is no longer functional. In leaving the city for the suburbs, upwardly mobile Jews, like other Americans, are suppressing their urban ethnic past, exchanging it for a luxurious and privileged, if sanitized, present.

In this novella Ron and Harriet, Neil and Brenda, mirror each other ironically. Similarly, the young Negro boy in the library echoes Neil's experiences. Aunt Gla-

THE SUBURBS OF FORGETFULNESS

dys and Uncle Max are poorer immigrant versions of Mr. and Mrs. Patimkin. As a result of these doublings the reader cannot focus on one character alone, but rather encounters a complex and fuller situation in which a range of roles and character types are deployed. Brenda's country-club world, for example, is paralleled by Ron's fraternity at Ohio State, a school noted more for its football team than its academic standards. Their frat song, "Goodbye, Columbus," expresses the nostalgia for the enclosed happy world of sports achievements. For Ron, leaving Columbus is like Brenda's leaving the Patimkin sheltered, suburban home for the dangerous, anonymous city. Neil's anger and confusion are mirrored in Aunt Gladys's response to his courtship of the country-club girl from Short Hills, and are echoed in Mr. and Mrs. Patimkin's reactions to Brenda's wants and desires.

Like Neil, Brenda is ambivalent about her world. She quarrels with her mother, who treats her in the no-nonsense style of Aunt Gladys. Brenda observes the way her mother and father spoil Julie; she resents her mother's disapproval but is quick to get her father to buy her all the things—especially elegant clothes—she wants. Independent and strong-minded, Brenda is eager to succeed both in sports and academic life; like her father and Neil and unlike her brother, she seizes all her opportunities. Like Neil, Brenda constantly thinks about the meaning of her situation. Unlike Neil, she has put aside the expectations traditional Jewish families have for their children and wants to chart her own way. Her behavior, however, sometimes makes her appear like a girl with a "finishing school" frame of mind.

Despite the fact that Neil is the narrator of this tale, Brenda emerges as a more complex character than he is ready to acknowledge. By contrast with the other women in the stories that make up *Goodbye, Columbus*, she is the most liberated, sexually and socially, the most intelligent, and the one most able to combine her Jewish heritage and American possibility. The surprise with which Neil registers her words reveals how accurately and fully Roth has articulated the power of the new American-Jewish girl. Brenda is not the stereotypical Jewish-American princess of contemporary American folklore (with anti-Semitic overtones, as it has become an entire category of ethnic slurs and jokes);—that is a role her sister Julie will come to fulfill. Rather, Brenda is a figure of the fullness of American female possibility. She is the potentially liberated, new woman of the twentieth century, presented (and this is an indication of the power of Roth's work) through the eyes of a man who comes to challenge but stays to admire.

Despite their suburban home the Patimkins have not been able to change their urban Jewish linguistic usage. All of them are voluble; none of them feels threatened by Neil's verbal aggressiveness. Like Brenda, they can match him line for witty line. They make a theatrical experience of everything, whether it

THE SUBURBS OF FORGETFULNESS

is Brenda's seduction of Neil at the swimming pool or the phone call for Ron from Harriet that brings dinner to an abrupt end and galvanizes everyone into action. Their linguistic virtuosity, like everything else they do, has a rich surplus; like their personal energy, they glory in its excess. For them the pleasure is in the overdoing. Early in the novel when Neil looks in the refrigerator in the Patimkin home he registers the power of abundance and affluence. "I opened the door of the old refrigerator; it was not empty. No longer did it hold butter, eggs, herring in cream sauce, ginger ale, tuna fish salad, an occasional corsage—rather it was heaped with fruit, shelves swelled with it, every color, every texture, and hidden within, every kind of pit." This is not a city icebox, stocked with the few concessions to American supermarkets Aunt Gladys makes, but a transformed fridge that holds the promise of America for the Jews:

There were greengage plums, black plums, red plums, apricots, nectarines, peaches, long horns of grapes, black, yellow, red, and cherries, cherries flowing out of boxes and staining everything scarlet. And there were melons—cantaloupes and honeydews—and on the top shelf, half of a huge watermelon, a thin sheet of wax paper clinging to its bare red face like a wet lip (43).

The sensuality and richness of this description of a Jew-ish-American household by an American-Jewish writer reveal that the Jews are at home in this new world. Just as Roth can write English as well as the classic English writers, so Jews can live as well as any other Americans. Roth will find the words to represent the experiences of this newly emergent ethnic American community. "Oh Patimkin! Fruit grew in their refrigerator and sporting goods dropped from their trees" (43). This section of the novella, in which Neil discovers the cornucopia in the Patimkin basement, concludes with Brenda and Neil making love for the first time.

In the next section, Neil thinks only of Brenda and, at work, pays attention to the needs of the young black boy, making sure he can look at the sensual pictures of Gauguin's Tahiti. Neil and Brenda briefly discuss his parents and his work: Brenda pointedly asks him whether he expects to make a career of the library. Though these are disturbing developments, they do not at this point puncture the sexual euphoria which envelops Neil and Brenda. Neil announces that he is spending his summer vacation at the Patimkin's home; his stay will extend through Labor Day.

One day Neil journeys to the "heart of the Negro section of Newark," where Patimkin Kitchen and Bathroom Sinks is located. Years ago, Neil muses, at the height of the great Jewish immigration, this had been the Jewish section of town, with its spicy-smelling ethnic stores and Turkish baths. Thinking about the waves of immigrants passing through this city, Neil wonders who will succeed "the Negroes" (90–91). Ron now works for his father, and Neil and Mr. Patimkin have a

THE SUBURBS OF FORGETFULNESS

brief conversation in which Brenda's father comments on Ron's inability, so essential to success in business, to make the most of small advantages. "Here you need a little of the *gonif* in you. You know that that means?" and to Neil's response, "Thief," Mr. Patimkin comments approvingly: "You know more than my own kids. They're *goyim*, my kids, that's how much they understand"; (94). In the intimacy of the talk and the approval which Mr. Patimkin gives Neil for his knowledge of the old ways, the scene suggests he is the true heir to the business—the potential son-in-law who can do what the Americanized son cannot. The encounter of Neil and Brenda thus serves to bridge the values of the immigrant Jewish past and the American future.

As their relationship continues, Neil asserts himself with Brenda; however, he does not ask her to marry him but rather to get a diaphragm. Brenda's response is to claim that Neil is only interested in his own pleasure. Nevertheless, she accedes to his request. As Neil waits for Brenda to emerge from the doctor's office, he goes into a church and muses about his life. He thinks about his eagerness to be a winner and imagines Brenda is the prize. "It was an ingenious meditation, and suddenly I felt ashamed. I got up and walked outside, and the noise of Fifth Avenue met me with an answer: Which prize do you think, *schmuck?* Gold dinnerware, sporting-goods trees, Patimkin Sink, Bonwit Teller"— and Neil reverts to the tough, street-smart kid who won't let anyone, not even himself, get away with anything. "And then I saw Brenda coming out of the Squibb Building. She carried nothing with her, like a woman who's only been window shopping, and for a moment I was glad that in the end she had disobeyed my desire." But Brenda surprises Neil. "'Where is it?' I said. . . . At last she said, 'I'm wearing it'" (100–01). The insouciance with which she manages this transaction expresses her ease and habit of control; by contrast with Neil's identity crisis Brenda, even though she is younger, yet knows who she is.

Later, when Mrs. Patimkin discovers the diaphragm and confronts Brenda with it, the ensuing quarrel of the two lovers leads to the breakup of their relationship. Neil accuses Brenda of purposely leaving it where her mother would find it. Their argument about the diaphragm is again a displacement of the real question of responsibility for continuing (or ending) their relationship. Despite their seeming self-possession, neither Neil nor Brenda can deal with their situation. Reaching for a common future, they are too rooted in their different pasts. Their feelings lead them, but the nature of their emotions is brought into question. As the epigraph to the books suggests, "the heart" here is "only half a prophet." Personal profit is the other half of their relationship. Their hearts are not natural; they are managed.

What the characters of "Goodbye, Columbus" do not understand is that their push toward individual mobility and assimilation into the larger American culture

THE SUBURBS OF FORGETFULNESS

will also mean the transformation of their Jewish community. Unlike Bernard Malamud, who relocates the immigrant's Old World village in the American city, Philip Roth recognizes the new opportunities of American Jewish life. By contrast with Saul Bellow, who for the most part views these new opportunities as intellectual problems of thinking and reconceptualization, Roth focuses on them as part of the process of growing up. Education and the family are his central themes as he explores the ways in which people negotiate everyday life, express their deepest feelings and values, and thereby imagine and invent their lives.

The summer comes to a close with the wedding of Ron and Harriet. Brenda's Uncle Leo regales Neil with an account of the heights of his sex life. The ritual moment of the gathering of the clan serves to reveal the link between ecstatic sex and Jewish celebration. The rich talk of these exuberant characters becomes an index of their vitality and sexual intensity: Brenda's sharp practical wit, and Uncle Leo's anecdotes echo Aunt Gladys's vivid phrases with their Yiddish inflection. Neil, in whom everyone now confides, draws out their linguistic energy. The affluent Patimkins celebrate the marriage of their firstborn son by overdoing things in good American, rather than strictly Jewish, style. Their excess marks the exuberance with which they have chosen to be Americans. But their Jewish energy shapes their Americanness, expressed in the *chutzpa*—the nerve—with which they address the possibilities of life.

As adventurers the Patimkins are infectious. They seduce the reader into sharing in their daring feats of life and language.

Near the end of the evening, Brenda, who'd been drinking champagne like her Uncle Leo, did a Rita Hayworth tango with herself, and Julie fell asleep on some ferns she'd whisked off the head table and made into a mattress at the end of the hall. I felt a numbness creep into my hard palate, and by three o'clock people were dancing in their coats, shoeless ladies were wrapping hunks of wedding cake in napkins for their children's lunch, and finally Gloria Feldman made her way over to our end of the table and said, freshly, "Well, our little Radcliffe smarty, what have *you* been doing all summer" (110).

Brenda's response reveals her ability to defend herself with her native wit and theatrically honed poise. "Growing a penis," she says. Her splendid punch line turns a put-down into a triumphant assertion of self. Like Neil's, her words give her an edge over everyone else. Her talk, like her sexual inventiveness, makes her the queen of this romantic world.

Despite Neil's willingness to follow Ron's example, the romance comes to a painful end in the autumn. Brenda goes back to Radcliffe, and Neil returns to the Newark Public Library and a promotion to head of the Reference Section. After much negotiation Neil agrees to go to Boston over Rosh Hashana, the Jewish New Year. In Boston, however, Neil and Brenda find it difficult to recover their summer intimacy. Instead of sexual encounter they are forced into their long-deferred conversation by the two letters Brenda has received from her parents after they discovered her diaphragm. The resulting quarrel ends up forcing each not only into self-justification but into inadvertent choosing of his and her own family, class, and home.

"I loved you, Brenda, so I cared."

"I loved *you*. That's why I got that damn thing in the first place."

And then we heard the tense in which we'd spoken and we settled back into ourselves and silence (134).

Returning to Newark, Neil asks himself the questions that might help him account for what has happened. He is left with the bitterness of his ambivalence. He arrives in Newark "just as the sun was rising on the first day of the Jewish New Year. I was back in plenty of time for work" (136). Instead of the old ritual of family and synagogue, or the newly discovered one of sexual fulfillment, Neil has only his unsatisfying job to which to devote himself.

The satire of "Goodbye, Columbus" follows the trajectory of the *Bildungsroman*. The events highlight the lessons Neil must learn about his American and his Jew-

ish identity. In bringing the values of the past to bear
on the present, Roth's satire implicitly recovers neglected values. Preserving a people's memory, he keeps
alive the possibility of a vital American Jewish historical
consciousness in the 1950s, a decade devoted to forgetfulness.[2]

"The Conversion of the Jews"

In the five short stories in *Goodbye, Columbus* Roth's
concerns as an American political satirist and as an eth-
nographic recorder of Jewish life work together. Moral
pattern, literary strategy, and rhetorical tactic link
American and Jewish themes, revealing them to be opposite sides of the same coin. Each of these stories
builds to a crisis in which the protagonist must acknowledge his Jewishness by taking a particular course of action. That recognition has major consequences for the
other characters and transforms the situation. Ironically, in each instance the Jewish course of action turns
out to be identical with, rather than opposed to, the
democratic, American choice.

In "The Conversion of the Jews" brash young Ozzie
Freedman cannot keep from asking questions in Hebrew school. Unlike his fellow classmates, who content
themselves with gestures and grimaces, Ozzie responds
to his teacher's sententious statements with pointed

queries. "Anyway, I asked [Rabbi] Binder," if God "could make all that in six days, and He could *pick* the six days he wanted right out of nowhere, why couldn't He let a woman have a baby without having intercourse" (141). This and similar questions get Ozzie into trouble: not only must he defend his intellectual exuberance to his friends, but his mother must come to school to meet with Rabbi Binder.

Ozzie finds the theological issues fascinating; unlike his elders, however, he does not privilege Jewish over American themes. For him they are both part of his inheritance as an American Jew. Thus he wants to know how the Jews can be the Chosen People if the Declaration of Independence claims all men are created equal. And when fifty-eight people are killed in a plane crash and his grandmother and mother pore over the lists to detect which of the victims were Jewish, Ozzie cannot help but raise the problem with Rabbi Binder. The rabbi's effort to deal with Ozzie's specific concerns by abstracting them into matters of "cultural unity and some other things" leads to a confrontation: Rabbi Binder yells at the boy, and Ozzie "shouted that he wished all fifty-eight were Jews." Even the chance to "think it over" in the rabbi's office for an hour does not convince Ozzie he was wrong in his conviction that God the Creator is all-powerful. Ozzie suspects that Rabbi Binder, like the seventy-one-year-old custodian of the synagogue who mumbles his prayers, has memorized the prayers but forgotten about God.

By contrast, Ozzie's deep religious feelings lead him to honor the Sabbath: "When his mother lit candles Ozzie felt there should be no noise; even breathing, if you could manage it, should be softened." Even though his mother is tired from work and her daily struggle as a widow, "when she lit candles she looked like something better; like a woman who knew momentarily that God could do anything" (143). But when Ozzie tells her that she will have to see Rabbi Binder again, this time about the confrontation over the plane crash, she slaps him. Shocked by the discovery that she does not share his view of God's power and presence, Ozzie cries through Sabbath dinner.

The day his mother is to come to Hebrew school, Ozzie and Rabbi Binder have another fight. Ozzie asks Rabbi Binder about God's power as creator, and Itzie gestures obscenely behind the rabbi's back, making the class burst into laughter. As the rabbi momentarily turns away, Ozzie yells at him, "You don't know anything about God!" (146), and the angered rabbi turns and slaps Ozzie, bringing blood from his nose. In the ensuing confusion Ozzie escapes to the roof of the synagogue, where he muses on the strange events that led him there. Down below, the adults misinterpret his actions; thinking that he will jump, they plead with him. Struck with his sudden power, Ozzie takes the opportunity to continue the theological discussion of God's power.

Ozzie Freedman's innocence makes him take literally what his teachers interpret allegorically and contextually. A marginal figure, an *isolato*, like so many classic American literary heroes, he does not participate in the conventions that limit the adult world. Like Huckleberry Finn, one of his literary ancestors, Ozzie the outsider thinks for himself. As a result his questions unintentionally subvert normative values and beliefs and threaten the social order of his elders. The violence which greets Ozzie's sincere desire for knowledge leads him to the discovery of the political dimensions of the social contract and the extent of his own isolation and marginality.

Like many Jewish communal leaders in the 1950s Rabbi Binder spends the greater part of his energies in separating what is Jewish from what is non-Jewish. As his name suggests, he is eager to bind his flock to their Jewish values; unfortunately that effort blinds him to the values that Americans, whether Jews or Christians, share.[3] Rabbi Binder views his rights as an American as circumscribed by his Jewishness, while Ozzie's actions reveal how vigorously he pursues his rights as an American citizen. There are no limits to what he asks about, and he will not accept the adult response that "it's always been that way." Roth dramatizes both the question and the hostile answer, for he knows that to ask an insecure young rabbi about central Christian dogma with the brash naïveté of the Jewish child is to provoke unthinking, even reactionary responses. The encounter between Rabbi Binder and Ozzie is not only a confrontation between two social unequals—in that case the adult would generally have the upper hand—but between two views of American citizenship. Ozzie's demand makes everyone accept the republican and democratic conditions of American life. Asking questions that are subversive, Ozzie exercises those rights acquired through the process of Jewish Emancipation—the political movement initiated by Napoleon in the aftermath of the French Revolution, which gave the Jews the rights of citizenship in the countries of the West—and that are part and parcel of the conditions making American pluralism possible. The irony of the title—"The Conversion of the Jews"—lies in the fact that the Jews are not here converted to Christianity but to the rights of American citizenship guaranteed to all by the American Constitution and the Declaration of Independence.

Much of the force of Roth's ironic tale depends upon parallel sources in American and Jewish culture that emphasize the power of the innocent child. What more American a subject than the outspoken, rebellious young boy; what more Jewish a subject than the smart, questioning student whose understanding far surpasses that of his elders. Ozzie unmasks the implicit arrangements by which adults, Jewish and non-Jewish, rationalize their situations. His innocence brings him to anger; he turns the conventional boundaries that supposedly shore up the individual identities of these adults against them. Unable to tolerate the compromises implied by this particular social arrangement, Ozzie—when he fortuitously gains the upper hand by threatening to hurl himself off the roof—forces his mother, Rabbi Binder, and all those listening to him to kneel. The title of the story expresses the acknowledgment Ozzie forces Rabbi Binder to make: God "can make a child without intercourse." Then "he made them all say they believed in Jesus Christ." Almost as an afterthought he adds, "Promise me, promise me you'll never hit anybody about God" (157–58). In this way Ozzie takes religion out of the private realm and makes it a public issue. Rabbi Binder is forced to acknowledge the interdependence of the religious beliefs of both Christian and Jew, which depend upon a similar kind of faith. In effect, they are different in degree rather than kind; they exist together in the same universe of discourse. This recognition is one that Rabbi Binder has steadfastly denied in response to Ozzie's clever queries. Rabbi Binder has separated religious from ethnic experience, limiting his moral explorations to what he thinks of as Jewish issues, while refusing to confront larger, more general questions about belief and faith. In "The Conversion of the Jews," Roth, the political satirist and Jewish ethnographer, shows the intertwining of religion, politics, and ethnicity.

"Defender of the Faith"

In the first-person narrative of "Defender of the Faith" Sergeant Nathan Marx recounts a confrontation he has had with Sheldon Grossbart, a private in his company and a fellow Jew, late in May, 1945, near the end of World War II. During the course of basic training at Camp Crowder, Missouri, Sheldon has made a point of contacting Marx, the new first sergeant. Playing on their common Jewish heritage, Sheldon begins by asking that he be allowed to celebrate the Sabbath. His requests pile up, and soon Marx discovers that Sheldon is seeking preferential treatment from a fellow Jew. These events are bracketed by a retrospective opening in which Marx muses about his experiences in combat in Europe and a concluding scene which looks toward combat in the Pacific. Together, dramatic confrontation and meditative retrospect and prospect make it possible for Marx to come to a decision about his identity as an American, Jew, and soldier.

Sergeant Marx finds himself caught between Grossbart's requests, which evoke the world of his own Jewish family with its warmth and disinclination to violence or the severity of military law, and the demands of his captain, who admires him "because of the ribbons on your chest, not because you had a hem stitched on your dick before you were old enough to even know you had one" (166). Marx soon finds he must represent the demands of the army and his captain to Grossbart and his

THE SUBURBS OF FORGETFULNESS

two Jewish sidekicks, while at the same time standing up for Jewish traditions and family life to Captain Barrett. Despite his effort to mediate between the two so as to honor both, Marx finds that Grossbart is taking advantage of him, and in his rage interferes with Grossbart's effort to be reassigned to New Jersey rather than the Pacific theater of operations. It is this act which leads to Marx's understanding of the ways in which he is a defender of the faith.

Marx's view of American life does not separate the responsibilities of the Jew from those of the American citizen. Sheldon Grossbart only sees the privileges he is being denied by military service and seeks to recover them by playing on the Jewishness he shares with Sergeant Nathan Marx. For him the ethnic connection is primary and overrules the more abstract, secondary loyalty of soldiers and citizens. In the course of the story Nathan is forced to choose between the Jewishness Grossbart insinuates should entitle him to privileges at the hands of his fellow Jew and a view of Judaism and Americanness as a set of mutual and overlapping obligations.

Nathan has fought against the Nazis in Europe; he has been decorated for bravery under fire. While he is held up to the recruits at the base as an example of someone who has earned his commander's respect, he is also razzed for his name and his Jewishness; it would be easy for him to choose ethnic solidarity over American citizenship. However, unlike Grossbart, Marx does not separate his Jewishness from his Americanness. Like Ozzie Freedman in "The Conversion of the Jews," Marx demands that both be fulfilled: Nathan Marx and Ozzie Freedman both demand that the Jew live up to the highest universal standards of justice and fairness. For Nathan it is not enough for Jews to fight the Nazis; because Jewish and American values overlap, the war must also be brought to a conclusion in the Pacific.

Both the central characters of "Defender of the Faith" are Jews. Nevertheless, their views of the obligations and responsibilities of modern American Jews diverge. Marx does not accept Grossbart's definition of the situation as "them against us." In an era in which the organized American Jewish community was emphasizing its ethnic solidarity, Nathan's exposure of Grossbart's pursuit of preferential treatment caused many readers to label the story anti-Semitic. For Marx, to shirk the fulfillment of one's duty as an American is to fail to fulfill a Jewish obligation as well. Thus, he repudiates Sheldon's charge that he is an anti-Semite because he does not help him escape assignment to combat in the Pacific.

The encounter between Grossbart and Marx is a struggle between two views of American Jewish life, realized as two different ways of seeing. In this story about the demands American military training placed on Jews near the end of World War II, the soldier's life is presented visually: roll call, discipline, and medals

THE SUBURBS OF FORGETFULNESS

take up much of the beginning of the story. What happens when a young Jewish soldier tries to avoid facing up to required basic military training appears as a sequence of brief encounters of small figures against a larger background. The European and Pacific theatres of combat bracket the theatrical space of Camp Crowder, in which these actors play out their roles. Grossbart's world is spatially limited; he is afraid of the open space of the military drill field. Marx's world encompasses the horizon as it takes into account the larger view of the conflict and the obligations of Jews and Americans.

"You Can't Tell a Man by the Song He Sings" and "Epstein"

Parallel visual contrasts also define the situation in the next two stories. The contrasting spaces in which events take place are carefully described. Setting and characterization are intertwined, as characters are placed in their social context by manners and dress. In "You Can't Tell a Man by the Song He Sings" classroom behavior becomes an index of social class; in "Epstein" a socialist button pinned to a teddy bear, baseball cards, a folk singer, a thin dress, stockings, and the absence of a coat on a chilly morning are details that mark the class positions and the historical commitments of differ-

UNDERSTANDING PHILIP ROTH

ent characters. In both stories such details define the historical moment in terms of the inflections of class, gender, and political allegiance of the fictional characters. These nuances of social position are encapsulated by the particular dialogue of each character, which locates him along the social spectrum. The plot generates encounters between characters from different groups, and the resulting confrontations bring these different linguistic habits and social manners, as they challenge the range of possibilities available, to a sharp focus.

In "You Can't Tell a Man by the Song He Sings" the friendship between Alberto Pelagutti, tough reform school kid, and the narrator cuts across class and ethnic lines. Despite their different attitudes to school and education they bond with the other boys to defeat Mr. Russo, the "occupations" teacher, by forcing him to let them sing "The Star Spangled Banner" in the middle of class. This episode serves as the context for the discovery that the system that has marked Albie as an ex-con has done the same for their teacher, Mr. Russo, blacklisting him as a communist. By the end of the story the narrator realizes that the telltale index cards which indelibly record past mistakes will catch up not only with Albie, the student, but even more shockingly with their teacher. The story ends by making the reader ask with the narrator whether "a man's history is his fate."

The same pattern of discovery informs the farcical "Epstein." Here the story turns on an irritation Ep-

THE SUBURBS OF FORGETFULNESS

stein's wife discovers on his penis, the result of an illicit sexual encounter with a widow across the street. Encouraged by her daughter's sexual encounter with his nephew, which Epstein has accidentally seen, he seduces Ida Kaufman. When his wife, Goldie, discovers the irritation, she is convinced he has always been an unfaithful, philandering husband, and she demands a divorce—something unheard of in their Jewish neighborhood. As he tries to escape from her recriminations by seeking solace with Ida, Epstein collapses in her bedroom. His heart attack reconciles his wife to him. The young doctor in the ambulance assures Goldie it is not syphilis that Epstein has but "an irritation" that can be cured.

All of these stories begin with an encounter of people of unequal status. Then they progress to a possible friendship between them, and move to a tumultuous climax when their differing expectations clash head-on. In each case a secret is revealed that brings the original encounter full circle. Each story presents the conflict visually, so that "The Conversion of the Jews," for example, has Ozzie on top of a building demanding that his mother, friends, and rabbi kneel to keep him from jumping off. The vertical axis in this story, with Ozzie on top and Rabbi Binder kneeling below, reverses the expected social hierarchy.

"Eli, the Fanatic"

The structural principle of reversal is also at work in "Eli, the Fanatic," the first major story about the Holocaust written by an American writer after the first wave of reporting that succeeded the end of World War II had come to a close. Roth observed that most American Jews in the decade and a half following the end of the war embraced the process of suburbanization and assimilation. In 1959 he probed the repressed shame and guilt Western Jews felt about the Holocaust, while other distinguished American Jewish writers did not deal with it as a major subject for almost another decade.

As a satirist Roth understands the importance of community life and communal norms: they are the necessary conditions for satire. In the era of the disintegration of urban neighborhoods and communities Roth knows that these norms exist for the most part as past events that have been repressed. In "Eli, the Fanatic" the arrival of the group of Holocaust survivors who organize a Yeshivah (a traditional school of advanced Jewish learning) in one of the large old houses in the peaceful suburb of Woodenton disturbs its placid surface. The traditional long black cloak of the Hasidic Jew which one of the survivors wears provokes the assimilating Jews of the town, as if it were a lure to bring them out of their hiding places. The satire of the story, like its comedy, derives from the excessive feelings this inno-

THE SUBURBS OF FORGETFULNESS

cent figure stirs up. He arouses little comment among the other townspeople; to the Jews he is a red flag.

In the course of the story this survivor becomes the fictional double of Eli Peck, a young lawyer with a history of mental illness, who has been asked by his fellow Jews in Woodenton to force the survivors to close the Yeshivah and leave. The Jews have discovered that it is against the zoning laws to run a school in that area of town. After a long day of work in the city Eli confronts the head of the Yeshivah, Leo Tzuref, with that fact, only to be told that the nineteen people who are involved are all family members and live there. Leo's expressive body language forces Eli into unexpected negotiations. Eli finds himself trying to justify the concerns of his Jewish neighbors to Tzuref—whose name echoes both the Yiddish word for trouble, *tsuris,* and the Hebrew word for participation, joining, *(le)tsaref*—and the Yeshivah's needs to the Jews of Woodenton.

Eli's buddies are dismayed. Though they have left the city where such things happen for the quiet suburb, the disturbing city experiences that throw all kinds of people together every day have now followed them to Woodenton. Eli's effort to persuade them that the disturbances that have provoked them, especially the wandering figure in the long black cloak and hat from the Yeshivah, will shortly cease does not convince them. Pursuing his effort at mediation, Eli sends the survivor two of his suits, discovering in the process that his wife, Miriam, who is in her ninth month of pregnancy with their first child, sides fully with the other Jews of Woodenton. However, Eli's strategy seems to work: now the survivor wears Eli's green suit as he strolls about town and is no longer recognizable as different from all the other people of Woodenton. Eli begins to think of him as "greenie"; the nickname is not only descriptive of his suit, but as well evokes "greenhorn," the traditional word for the American Jewish immigrant compounded out of Yiddish and late-nineteenth-century American English usage. When Miriam goes into labor, Eli takes her to the hospital. Returning home, he finds that the survivor has sent him the black suit of clothes, including the ritual fringed undergarment of *tzitzit* in exchange.

Eli is irresistibly drawn to these clothes, finally putting them on and going to meet the "greenie" to show him what he looks like in the long black cloak, suit, hat, and fringed undergarment. Their meeting echoes a climactic moment in Sholem Aleichem's classic story "On Account of a Hat," in which the main character cannot recognize himself in a mirror because he has put on an officer's cap by mistake: "And then Eli had the strange notion that he was two people. Or that he was one person wearing two suits" (289). The encounter leads Eli to an understanding of some of the experiences of the Holocaust survivor, of which Tzuref has spoken earlier. Identifying with him, Eli has a revelation. Now he becomes the committed Jew—the "fanatic" of the title of the story, living up to "Eli," which means "my God"

THE SUBURBS OF FORGETFULNESS

in classical Hebrew and was the name of the high priest of the Temple in 1 Samuel. In his black Hasidic traditional clothing Eli strolls deliberately through the town, making visible to his Jewish friends and neighbors the experiences they want to banish and have repressed in their hearts. As the cars screech to a stop and people call his name, Eli discovers his identity: "he knew who he was down to his marrow—they were telling him. Eli Peck. He wanted to say it a thousand times, a million times, he would walk forever in that black suit, as adults whispered of his strangeness and children made 'Shame . . . shame' with their fingers" (293). Then Eli walks to the hospital to see his newborn son. Looking at him through the glass wall that separates them, he imagines himself cutting down the suit for his son to wear, "whether the kid liked it or not!" (297), thereby defining Jewish tradition through this image of clothing.

The black suit accumulates additional meanings in the course of the story. His wife as well as his friends become convinced that Eli has had another attack of mental illness and call for Dr. Eckman, the psychiatrist, who has been a threatening presence in his life. Eli feels very clear about who he is for the first time in his life; his friends, however, cannot acknowledge his discovery. His sense of having come home at last makes no sense to them, for unlike Eli they do not pursue issues to their conclusions, preferring instead to keep things stable and "normal" by banishing unwanted cultural and personal memories. As the story concludes, Eli is grabbed by two interns, who call him rabbi at the same time that they administer a sedative: "The drug calmed his soul, but did not touch it down where the blackness had reached" (298).[4] The blackness with which the story ends becomes a complex image: it is both the traditional suit of clothes as an emblem of tradition which clothes the human being, and the horror of the Holocaust. It also brings into bold relief the shabbiness of the response of the other Jews of Woodenton, eliciting their self-hatred and fear. Thus, "Eli, the Fanatic" focuses on the self-imposed censorship of American suburban Jewish life, which depends upon the refusal to acknowledge the links between individual American Jews and the larger community of Jews, the *klal yisroel*—that is, the entire people of Israel. The recurring image of blackness builds in this story into a judgment of what the Jews of Woodenton want to repress.

"Eli, the Fanatic" is a cautionary fable about what happened in the 1950s to Jews as they tried to disappear into the suburbs and abandon their communal life. When the young Holocaust survivor moves through Woodenton in his long Hasidic black coat, the response of the Jewish suburb to the appearance of someone in the traditional clothing of religious Jews reveals that the effort to forget extends to the visible marks of their historic meaning. The name of their town—Woodenton—precisely expresses what they have done in anesthetizing themselves against the shocks of modern Jewish history.

THE SUBURBS OF FORGETFULNESS

Notes

1. Roth, *Goodbye, Columbus* (Boston: Houghton Mifflin, 1959) 3. Further references will be noted parenthetically.

2. The title of this chapter echoes that of an important essay by our late colleague, Professor Joseph H. Silverman.

3. For further discussion of the differences between Rabbi Binder and Ozzie, see Will Herberg, *Protestant, Catholic, Jew: An Essay in American Religious Sociology* (Garden City, NY: Doubleday, 1956), and J. M. Cuddihy, *The Ordeal of Civility: Freud, Marx, Levi-Strauss, and the Jewish Struggle with Modernity* (New York: Basic Books, 1974).

4. Roth made significant revisions to the ending of this story in the second edition, which is quoted here.

American Innocence/ American Anger: *Letting Go* (1962); *When She Was Good* (1967)

In his first two full-length novels Philip Roth captures the turns of phrase, the accents and intonations of his characters, and the nuances of their social world with the uncanny accuracy that has continued to characterize his work throughout his career. Whether they are second-generation Jews from New York or Chicago, or midwestern immigrants from small-town America who move to the metropolis, the difference between their expectations and their achievements forms the subject of much of his satire. On the margins of society, his protagonists begin their careers as innocents but turn quickly into angry heroes and heroines. Thus, the sociological dimension of his fiction leads to the representation of the psychological dynamic of his characters' lives.

AMERICAN INNOCENCE/AMERICAN ANGER

Letting Go

Though many of the characters in *Letting Go* travel home to New York and its suburbs, most of the action takes place in and around Hyde Park and the University of Chicago. Chicago lives up to its nickname of Windy City, its variable weather serving to counterpoint the moods of the novels' characters. The major characters travel within the city, but only its narrator, Gabe, and his friend, Martha, savor its human and architectural diversity. A wide range of minor characters, from many different ethnic groups and social classes, make their appearances, and Roth renders their different ways of using English so accurately that the novel can be read as a linguistic atlas. This urban interaction of different classes, ethnic groups, folk and high cultures, is drawn from the experiences Roth garnered first as a graduate student at the University of Chicago and then as a part-time faculty member there. *Letting Go* echoes Chicago traditions of civic concern, urban planning, and city pride articulated by Louis Wirth, Robert Park, and Jane Addams.

Gabe Wallach, the narrator of *Letting Go*, is a disciplined and hard-working English instructor at the University of Chicago in the late 1950s. Despite his professional success he is directionless and troubled. He has internalized the cultural malaise of an America sick with the surfeit of suburban consumerism and spiritual loss. The question of meaning—"what is the point of it all"—

underlies everything he does. Rather than risking himself by entering into a relationship with a woman, Gabe lives vicariously through Paul Herz, who is also an English instructor. Both are Jewish and grew up in New York, though Paul comes from a less-well-to-do family. A graduate student and instructor, Paul thinks of himself as a novelist in training. In keeping with Gabe's failures, his double, Paul is unable to complete the manuscript of his novel. At least in part this is due to the financial difficulties of an early marriage to Libby, whom he supports and who is often too sickly to work.

In *Letting Go* Roth explores the permutations of love, success, and the problems of personal identity and communal origins in ways that echo the personal, professional, and psychosexual dilemmas of "Goodbye, Columbus." However, instead of the gutsy strength and daring of adventurers like Neil and Brenda, Paul and Libby Herz have the psychic and social fragility of survivors. Their economic and social deprivation come to a focus in their inability to have children, and the plot of the story turns on the process of adoption which they initiate.

Because Libby is not Jewish, Paul's parents, particularly his father, have disowned him, as Libby's Christian parents have disowned her for marrying Paul. Rather than fulfilling the liberal promise of a richer and fuller secular life, beyond the constrictive bounds of clan and tribe, their marriage impoverishes them. It deprives them culturally, financially, and spiritually, cutting them off from family and community, and ultimately from themselves and each other.

Like Paul, Libby can also be read as a shadow figure for Gabe. Libby and Gabe share a brief interlude together which provides sexual fantasy material for both of them. They are further linked by complementary functions: Libby embodies the malaise which engenders the questions about the meaning of life Gabe can't quite bring himself to ask. These questions—What should one do? What for? What is the point of it all?—haunt her meandering existence. And it is her position in the novel as directionless, powerless, and without viable alternatives outside her marriage which reveals the sense of futility at the heart of *Letting Go* and of the deracinated characters and communityless milieu Roth so accurately depicts.

In the meantime Gabe gets halfheartedly involved with several women. After a frantic love affair with a student, which he ends when he discovers the extent of her dependency on him, Gabe is attracted to a more mature woman, Martha Regenhart. Their relationship, the most compelling part of the novel, mirrors that of Neil and Brenda in "Goodbye, Columbus," but with the class situation reversed. Gabe's father, like Brenda's, is successful, and like Brenda, Gabe has had everything he could possibly want. Martha, more like Neil, has had to struggle and, now that she is divorced, to raise and provide for her two children as a single parent. But Martha, unlike her male counterpart, Neil, is tempted into the relationship not so much by the signs of material comfort as by the hope of emotional stability and support. Gabe moves in with Martha and her two children, but he is never really willing, as she can see only too well, to make a real commitment to her. Their interfaith relationship, though potentially enriching where Libby and Paul's is arid and stultifying, terminates abruptly because of Gabe's "suburban" limitations: his alienation from others and, finally, from himself.

The novel begins with three epigraphs which point to the seriousness of its intent. The first epigraph, by Thomas Mann, focuses on the "guileless unrealism of our youth," followed by Simone Weil's comment on the unrealistic expectations men have of women; the third quotes the poet Wallace Stevens on the complex relationship of sons and fathers. Together they delineate the novel's major themes. The first section, "Debts and Sorrows," begins with the last letter Gabe's mother has written to him before her death and traces the conflicting messages Gabe has received from his parents. In a note which Gabe gets while in the army his father points out the difficulties of life. Gabe's mother, on the other hand, wishes him to learn what it is to be "Very Decent to People." When his father's note arrives announcing her death and enclosing his mother's letter, Gabe—as if enacting his mother's message—is reading Henry James, whose novels center on social decorum, and slips the letter into *The Portrait of a Lady*. In retrospect this action becomes for him an emblem of the impossibility of choosing between the poles of mother and father when, in fact, both have helped to form him.

A year later, in graduate school at the University of Iowa, Gabe lends the book to Paul Herz, a fellow student. Soon afterward, Gabe is called by Libby Herz to help rescue Paul, whose car has broken down; the James novel and hidden letter which Libby reads and discusses with Gabe become the vehicle for the continuing relationship between them. At the end of this section Gabe helps arrange for Paul to teach at the University of Chicago. He receives a letter of thanks from Libby that he then places into *The Portrait of a Lady* along with the letter from his mother.

The next section, entitled "Paul Loves Libby," focuses on the Herzes, their families, their marriage, and their struggle to function as a couple. It is a realistic account of life on the edge of the academic profession.[1] Libby is often sick; Paul is solicitous, hard-working, caring—and somehow unable to make love to her. Both have been disowned by their families for their marriage, and both are therefore all the more determined to make their relationship succeed. Gabe's account of their habits is an effort to sort out his feelings for them and find out whether or not he loves Libby. But at the same time his constant dwelling on their situation is a way to avoid making his own commitments. Gabe realizes that his efforts to live up to his mother's injunction and be decent to everyone often keep him from realizing what they really want. As a result, he constantly says and does the wrong thing.

In section 3, "The Power of Thanksgiving," none of the characters is satisfied by the traditional feast, an indication of the inability to fulfill a familial role. The struggle of the sons to live up to their fathers' expectations interferes with their relationships, as Roth develops a subtle and deepening portrayal of unresolved oedipal tensions. Gabe flies to New York to be with his father, a lonely widower who has just returned from a trip to Europe with a new friend, Mrs. Fay Silberman, a widow whom he plans to marry. His father is eager for Gabe's approval; but when Gabe discovers Fay drunk in the kitchen he can hardly follow his dead mother's urgings and be civil to his future stepmother.

As his father announces his engagement to Fay, Gabe recalls his promise to Libby to inform Paul's family; they had broken off all contact after the marriage; and Gabe now flees from his father's house to Brooklyn to see Libby's in-laws, in whom he recognizes much of Paul. Roth parallels Gabe's feelings for Paul and Libby and the progress of his relationship with Martha Regenhart, whose invitation to Thanksgiving dinner he'd turned down in order to spend the day in New York with his father. Like a film director turning the camera-eye from one member of the scene to the other, Roth also changes the narrative focus of the novel to reveal the older Jewish generation's desire for acceptance by their younger, more American children. Wondering what families are about, a disturbed Gabe calls Martha Regenhart, only to interrupt her in an intimate moment. Her lawyer, Sid Jaffe, has just proposed marriage to her, and Gabe's call breaks into their embrace.

Whatever he touches, Gabe now disturbs. Entangled in many relationships and complicated feelings, which he is having increasing difficulty sorting out, Gabe struggles to find a center for his life. Upon his return to Chicago, he witnesses an intimate scene between Paul and Libby. She has gotten a job as secretary to the Dean, but is having trouble with it. On the verge of a collapse, she cries to Paul that she would like "a baby or a dog or a TV."[2] But when Gabe intervenes and shouts out to Paul to give Libby what she wants, she turns on him, blaming herself for their failure to have children. (Earlier Paul has been shown refusing to have sexual intercourse with Libby, a part of their relationship Gabe can only guess at.) Rebuffed by both, Gabe leaves to keep his date with Martha. As the result of a series of coincidences, their dinner will lead him to move in with her, as Martha becomes a temporary though ultimately unsatisfying anchor for an increasingly disturbed Gabe.

In the fourth section, "Three Women," Gabe seeks to help Libby and Paul adopt a child by making contact with Theresa, a pregnant, unmarried waitress with whom Martha works and whom she has tried to help. Gabe believes he owes the effort to Libby and Paul and is convinced that he, unlike anyone else, can help them succeed. Entangled by friendship and fantasy, he does not see himself as a meddler. Gabe decides he is becoming a more responsible adult and participates in Martha's management of her household and the raising of her two children, and is accepted by them. When her ex-husband returns, married, to claim the children and take them to the luxury of a Long Island home, Gabe helps to solace Martha. She reluctantly decides not to let her love for the children get in the way of the greater financial stability their father can offer.

In "Children and Men," the novel's fifth section, Gabe's feelings for Martha and Libby intertwine. Martha and Gabe have a summer together in Chicago. In Long Island her children, about whom she thinks constantly, enjoy a newfound material abundance, though they fear their father, who is an alcoholic, and begin to feel their stepmother's strength despite her tentativeness. By the end of the summer the relationship between Gabe and Martha begins to fray. Gabe visits his father, who is no longer sure he wants to marry Fay Silberman, though she has stopped drinking. The summer comes to a difficult end with a freak accident in which Martha's son is killed, pushed out of his bunk bed by his sister. As the chapter ends, it balances the death of Martha's child with the birth of Theresa's. Gabe decides to take responsibility for both Martha and Libby, and becomes "The Mad Crusader" of the sixth section of the novel.

AMERICAN INNOCENCE/AMERICAN ANGER

In the midst of his guilt and dissatisfaction with his marriage, Paul Herz flies East to see his estranged, now dying father. He stays with his uncle Asher, an artist, who lives a bohemian life as the family renegade. Asher has an odd relationship with an Asian woman who lives with him. He asks nothing from the people he knows, expects nothing, does only what he can, and takes only what is explicitly offered, living in accordance with an unarticulated set of Zen principles. Asher is Paul's opposite, and tries to talk to Paul about relinquishing his deep and perhaps misplaced, even obsessive sense of caring, so that he can "let go." Paul tells Asher, whose Hebrew name means the fortunate, satisfied one, that he is going to leave Libby and will not see his father before he dies. Asher does go to the funeral, but Paul refuses, claiming he must spend time looking for a job in New York instead, so that he can leave Chicago and Libby behind. Within an hour of his venturing forth, however, he is hiding in the bushes at the cemetery, observing the mourners at his father's funeral. Afterward, he returns to Chicago and Libby.

The last section, "Letting Go," brings the different strands of the plot together in Gabe's frenetic efforts to solve the Herzes' problems. Rather than confront his failure with Martha, Gabe displaces his emotions onto his married friends, especially Libby's desire to adopt a child in a neurotic attempt to save herself and her marriage. These overwhelming dilemmas lead Gabe out of his manageable middle-class realm into the harsh emotional, financial, sexual, and spiritual choices of Theresa's world. In their distorting mirror, Gabe confronts the problem of the comfortable meaninglessness of his own life.

In *Letting Go* Roth introduces issues and themes that recur throughout much of his work: the difficulties of being a Jewish son amid the claustrophobia of parental love; self-absorption and the difficulty of relationship; ethnicity, assimilation, intermarriage, and community; the privileges of class and the poverty of caste; angst and anxiety, moral responsibility and ethical choice; in addition to the self-reflexive concerns of authority and authorship, voice and form. Whether or not Gabe faces up to the reasons why he has become so deeply involved in the lives of Libby and Paul Herz and been unable to commit himself to a relationship with a woman remains unanswered at the conclusion of the novel. Given its reflective, retrospective tone and the separation of its two plot lines—Gabe's friendship with Libby and Paul, and his relationship with Martha, which echo the division of Gabe's personality into the different inheritances of his mother and father—no fuller resolution may be possible.

When She Was Good

When She Was Good is the only one of Roth's novels set in small-town midwestern America. There are no Jewish characters in it. The novel begins with the desire

AMERICAN INNOCENCE/AMERICAN ANGER

of Willard Carroll "to be civilized" and his plan to "travel all the way down to Chicago to find out" how to achieve it. None of the characters, however, ever manages to get there: the geography that defines their lives also articulates their hopes and failures. These midwesterners are migrants, moving from town to town in search of future happiness as restlessly as any immigrants. Roth's third work of fiction focuses on the impotent rage under the seemingly placid surface of the most ordinary American lives. Its careful third-person narration tracks the relationship between the Norman Rockwell surface and the nightmare the characters, especially its women, live every day. This pattern of oppression and quiet desperation turns out, as first noted by Thoreau, to be the heart of the American dream.

Roth dramatizes this experience by capturing the turns of phrase of these people. His narrative voice allows for the mimetic representation of their language. Marking the midwestern towns of *When She Was Good* by their turns of phrase, Roth maps the varied range of American English in the 1950s and 1960s. Bernard Rodgers notes that this book places Roth in the naturalistic tradition of Norris, Crane, Dreiser, and Sinclair Lewis.[3] Yet at the same time Roth renders the uneventful lives of his characters in an American idiom resonant with European overtones. Coping with the utter boredom of everyday American life, Lucy Nelson, as Sanford Pinsker argues in "'The Comedy That Hoits,'" is an American Madame Bovary.[4]

UNDERSTANDING PHILIP ROTH

In *When She Was Good*, as is the case in *Letting Go*, no one is happy, and no one seems to have the slightest notion how to change or make things any different. The system of exchange in which all participate as sexual, financial, parental, filial, and educational actors allows characters to choose their roles but not to redefine or transform them. All are oppressed by the narrow range of possibility. Women must get married; men will be irresponsible and ineffective; the community must keep people in their places: the status quo must be maintained. The male characters who surround the women and define the limits of their possibilities also judge them. As a result the women are deemed incompetent by petty men who constantly take advantage of them. The hope of freedom is extended while the possibility of living a larger, enriching life is squelched. These characters live in a classic double bind.[5]

Like Ozzie Freedman in "The Conversion of the Jews," Lucy Nelson is an *isolato*. Her marginality allows her to see the adult conventions of the world of *When She Was Good* more clearly than anyone else. Her innocence makes her take literally what parents, teachers, and friends interpret symbolically. Like many classic American literary heroes she does not participate in the conventions that limit the adult world. Rather, Lucy thinks for herself. As a result, her unintentionally subversive questions and behavior, like Ozzie's questions about normative values and beliefs, threaten the social order of her elders.

AMERICAN INNOCENCE/AMERICAN ANGER

What Lucy discovers is that as a woman she is pre-destined to be a victim. The two generations of women who precede her in *When She Was Good* accept their status. She does not. Lucy does, however, decide to be "very very good" as a way of realizing her hopes and desires. But, like the girl in the nursery rhyme, when she is bad—that is, when she uncovers the truths of her situation first as a pregnant, unwed mother-to-be and then as an abused wife who is taken for granted by everyone—she fulfills the rest of the rhyme: "When she was bad, she was horrid." As in Ozzie's case her inno-cence leads to anger, but it does not lead to effective action of the kind he was able to take.

Lucy Nelson is the angriest, and ultimately the most impotent, character in *When She Was Good*. More than any other figure in the novel, she perceives the hypocrisy of her family and her neighbors' lives. But she can discover no way to change either herself, her own circumstances, or anybody else. Lucy begins by trying to fulfill the roles she is offered. She ends up being horrid because she discovers that being good means turning the other cheek to ensure the mainte-nance of the status quo. Validating the way things are merely allows self-righteous and good-for-nothing men to have their way no matter how much it costs every-one—especially the psychic destruction of the women with whom they come in contact.

Like the heroine of *Madame Bovary*, Lucy grows up in an environment that keeps her from understanding the implications of what she sees in the small-town world in which she must make her way. Her sincerity collides with its gossipy values, and she does not know how to redefine her identity. Lucy thinks of herself alternately as victim and heroine, but in both roles she is cleverly manipulated by her husband, Roy. He takes advantage of the boredom on the surface of midwestern life to offer her a relationship that ends up defeating her. Roy is the obverse of Willard, Lucy's grandfather, whose defeatism and passivity determine his entire life experience. Willard is traumatized by the difficult conditions of his youth. He goes through life as if in a dream, hardly able to cope with everyday events, and unable to choose. Given that heritage, Lucy must deal with the weight of three generations in order to fashion a meaningful life for herself.

The problems Lucy has to face, and that destroy her, grow out of her powerless situation in the family. But the men in the novel treat her as if she has ultimate power. Caught in this double bind she steels herself and embraces first one side of the possibilities offered to her and then the other, but both are to no avail. Lucy lacks the nuanced possibilities of Ozzie. The confrontations she initiates as ways of demanding her rights as a citizen and a human being are evaded. Though she too questions authority, its social arrangements and bargains, she does not breathe the freer air of a new social possibility. Ozzie's daring leads to freedom, while Lucy's experience reveals what it meant for an average

AMERICAN INNOCENCE/AMERICAN ANGER

American woman to try to assert her rights before the rise of the contemporary women's movement. Lower-class women in this world do not enjoy the rights of citizenship either in their own family or in the larger society. There is no political world for them to function in and thereby define new possibilities for themselves. In such an environment Lucy strikes everyone as obsessive.

Like that of the classic American writers, Roth's work is filled with obsessive figures. Like Hawthorne and Melville, Roth writes of the difficulties of liberation, the power of its gestures as political and ethnic acts, their excesses and failures. Questioning the very possibility of individualism and autonomy, Roth implicitly asserts the claims of dependence. Lucy Nelson's strength is turned inward by the prevailing social conditions, and she becomes a victim of her own response to them as well as an example of their grim limitations.

In several public statements Roth has associated *When She Was Good* with *Portnoy's Complaint,* each of which, he claims, explores a familiar American family myth. In *Portnoy's Complaint* a Jewish son feels persecuted by an overprotective mother, while in *When She Was Good,* a Gentile daughter feels betrayed by an irresponsible alcoholic father.[6] The separation of the sexes in *When She Was Good* and *Portnoy's Complaint* destroys the possibility of effective communication between them. Like that of many classic American stories, which divide the worlds of men and women into utterly different spheres, these novels reveal the link between the male characters' victimization of female characters and their own profound feelings of male impotence. These are family patterns that in different inflections will recur in Roth's later novels.

Notes

1. Paul and Libby Herz, Theodore Solotaroff claims, are modeled in part on his wife and himself when they were graduate student friends of Roth's. Solotaroff is somewhat resentful of the liberties Roth took with their family life; see Solotaroff, "Philip Roth: A Personal View," *Critical Essays on Philip Roth*, ed. Sanford Pinsker (Boston: Hall, 1982) 133–48.

2. Roth, *Letting Go* (New York: Random House, 1962) 246. Further references will be noted parenthetically.

3. Bernard F. Rodgers, Jr., *Philip Roth* (Boston: Twayne, 1978), 66.

4. Sanford Pinsker, *"The Comedy That Hoits": An Essay on the Fiction of Philip Roth* (Columbia: University of Missouri Press, 1975), 43.

5. Judith Paterson Jones and Guinevera A. Nance, *Philip Roth* (New York: Ungar, 1981) 53ff.

6. Jones and Nance, 53.

CHAPTER FOUR

What DO Men Want, Dr. Roth? or, *Portnoy's Complaint* (1969)

It took seven years and several experimental narratives, as well as a play, for Roth to devise the final form of *Portnoy's Complaint*, his fourth work of fiction. Having begun to map the separate neighborhoods of sexuality and Jewishness in earlier works, in *Portnoy's Complaint* Roth brings them together in his discovery that Portnoy's "sexual feelings and his 'Jewish' feelings were just around the corner from each other."[1] Portnoy's childhood memories and adult fixations, as well as his attitudes to sex, family, and Jewish ethnicity, are woven together by the monologic form of the novel. Portnoy's manic talk spills out in the psychoanalyst's office as he reveals and simultaneously hides his emotions. Dramatizing the associative flow of feelings of his protagonist, as Portnoy expresses them in the process of speaking to his analyst, Roth gives a comic shape to the novel's disparate and even dissonant elements. *Portnoy's Complaint* might have been as somber an account as *Letting Go* or *When She Was Good*, for the expression of Alexander Portnoy's guilt has its tragic moments. But, Roth notes, that "sit-down comic" Franz Kafka showed him how to get "hold of guilt . . . as a comic idea"[2] and made it possible for Portnoy to emerge as a character at whom his audience laughs at the moment that they most sympathize with him.

Portnoy speaks not only to his therapist but to the average American caught in the same trials and tribulations brought on by the modern world's possibilities. In this monologue that is also a theatrical soliloquy Portnoy's obsessions move his complaint along without giving listener or therapist time to catch their breath. It is his whole personality, Portnoy as a psychic entity, not any particular action, that is center stage. "I'm living . . . in the middle of a Jewish joke,"[3] Portnoy complains, the desperation in his voice informing all the scenes and situations he narrates. In this novel, Roth demonstrates his mastery of the surface of the comedian's patter, representing its flow so effectively that what comes through is not so much the meaning of particular events as the qualities of Portnoy's speaking voice. Even his obvious and laughable inability to stop talking about himself and his situation become part of the novel's vivid immediacy and directness of address.

Portnoy's neurotic disorder makes its presence felt right from the beginning of the novel. Self-consciously and parodically Roth delimits his protagonist's condition on the first page by providing a dictionary definition of a disorder named after Portnoy "in which strongly-felt ethical and altruistic impulses are perpetually warring with extreme sexual longings, often of a perverse nature." Pushing the joke further, the mock psychological entry for "Portnoy's Complaint" continues by citing the definitive discussion of the case of Alexander Portnoy:

Spielvogel says: "Acts of exhibitionism, voyeurism, fetishism, autoeroticism and oral coitus are plentiful; as a consequence of the patient's 'morality,' however, neither fantasy nor act issues in genuine sexual gratification, but rather in overriding feelings of shame and the dread of retribution, particularly in the form of castration."

The citation to the fundamental article, "(Spielvogel, O., 'The Puzzled Penis'),", published, to be sure, in a German psychoanalytic journal, clinches the joke. Like *Moby-Dick*, which begins with encyclopedia references to giant whales in order to establish their novelistic plausibility, *Portnoy's Complaint* starts with a footnote to a learned journal to prove the existence of Portnoy's condition and of Portnoy himself. Once he is a "real person," the therapeutic situation of speaker and listener can be brought into play. Performing for each other, Portnoy and Spielvogel are also actors on the stage of personality (dis)order.

Like all therapeutic subjects Portnoy is trying to persuade his therapist of his view of reality. Bringing him into the "Jewish joke," Portnoy hopes to implicate

Spielvogel—and the reader who is also a listener in this novel—in his situation and thus validate his condition. Just as the whale becomes not only Ahab's difficulty but everyone's, so Portnoy's "puzzled penis," many of whose symptoms it is "believed by Spielvogel can be traced to the bonds obtaining in the mother-child relationship," becomes a shared public problem. Along with Portnoy, the monologist, and Spielvogel, the therapist, the reader participates in this game that has the shape of a joke and tall tale, and functions as a theatrical event.[4] Roth has been accused of betraying the secrets of the Jews to the anti-Semites. But it would be more accurate to say that the laughter of the hundreds of thousands of people who have read *Portnoy's Complaint* points to the art by which Roth makes ethnic insiders of everyone. By doing so, he makes the ethnicity of the Jews—the epitome of a minority people—central rather than marginal to American experience.

Portnoy, living in the middle of a Jewish joke, obsessed by "the outstanding producers and packagers of guilt in our times," as he calls his parents, is living nothing more than a somewhat exaggerated version of a normal American Jewish life. "Dr. Spielvogel," Portnoy cries out,

this is my life, my only life, and I'm living it in the middle of a Jewish joke! I am the son in the Jewish joke—*only it ain't no joke!* Please, who crippled us like this? Who made us so morbid and hysterical and weak? . . . Is this the Jewish suffering I used to hear so much about? Is this what has come down to me from the pogroms and the persecution? from the mockery and abuse bestowed by the *goyim* over these two thousand lovely years? Oh my secrets, my shame, my palpitations, my flushes, my sweats! (35–36).

This is Portnoy's version of Moses Herzog's complaint. Bellow's hero laments that all of Western civilization brought about his divorce; Portnoy that all of Western and Jewish history have led him to masturbation. Herzog's complaint makes readers smile at his naïve faith in ideas; the fears Roth's hero expresses leave them howling with laughter. "'Doctor, I can't stand any more being frightened like this over nothing! Bless me with manhood! Make me brave! Make me strong! Make me *whole!* Enough being a nice Jewish boy, publicly pleasing my parents while privately pulling my putz!'" (36). Portnoy here requests permission from Spielvogel to grow up and become an adult. He seeks release from his obsessive masturbation so that he may become a father, and be part of a family once more. It is clear, however, from his tone of voice and the narrated events that his guilt keeps him forever a child. His mother's seduction of him, for instance in the scene where she has him help her put on her stockings, has, Portnoy claims, a good deal to do with his inability to transfer his erotic feelings from himself to a woman. Thus

Portnoy's monologue enacts the oedipal comedy of family life.

Portnoy cannot help but think constantly about his situation. All thought, however, leads him obsessively back to himself and his problems of performance. Whatever he is doing serves as a foil to his own situation in the family home. Even Portnoy's comments about baseball reveal his obsession: a discussion of the differences between baseball and everyday life turns into a questioning of who he is. Baseball, he tells us, is a game bounded by very specific rules that define what the players do and give the players their rights. On the baseball field the center fielder—Portnoy's position—is a citizen, with clearly defined rights, privileges, and power, for

center field is like some observation post, a kind of control tower, where you are able to see everything and everyone, to understand what's happening the instant it happens, not only by the sound of the struck bat, but by the spark of movement that goes through the infielders in the first second that the ball comes flying at them; and once it gets beyond them, "It's mine," you call, "it's mine," and then after it you go. For in center field, if you can get to it, it *is* yours (68).

Portnoy's exclamation, "Thank God for center field," reveals what he is thinking about. His aria on the pleasures of baseball contrasts sharply with his own situ-

WHAT DO MEN WANT, DR. ROTH?

ation. "Oh, how unlike my home it is to be in center field, where no one will appropriate unto himself anything that I say is *mine*" (68).

Against this American ideal of baseball Portnoy measures the reality of his failures. "Unfortunately, I was too anxious a hitter to make the high school team—I swung and missed at bad pitches so often during the tryouts for the freshman squad that eventually the ironical coach took me aside and said, 'Sonny, are you sure you don't wear glasses?' and then sent me on my way" (69–70). Deprived of citizenship on the hardball diamond, Portnoy justifies himself by his success in softball. "But did I have form! did I have style! And in my playground softball league, where the ball came in just a little slower and a little bigger, I am the star I dreamed I might become for the whole school" (68). In this world citizenship must be earned. The ticket that provides the Jewish immigrant entry into the movie palace of American life does not endow him with the right to be a star of stage and screen. For that the linguistic mimicry and frantic comic energy of a Catskills comedian will not suffice. What is needed is the cool all-American ability of Jimmy Stewart and the poised skill of Joe DiMaggio, neither of which Portnoy as yet possesses.

Portnoy's Complaint sets the terms by which Philip Roth explores what it means to be Jewish and male in late-twentieth-century America. From this novel on, his tales focus on the struggle of his protagonists—urban, intellectual, second-generation American Jews—to define their masculinity over against a prototype of American maleness. That masculine ideal is desirable from the point of view of assimilating into the American mainstream, yet antithetical to certain elements in their ethnic makeup. Outwardly white and assimilated, inwardly Jewish men are more aware of their differences from American mainstream males than their similarities. Their differences are most pronounced in relation to gender characterization. Thus, for the Roth hero, the nexus of Jewishness and masculinity is crucial yet paradoxical. Jewishness contributes what the Roth hero most respects and yet most loathes in himself—that quality which makes him at one and the same time both superior and inferior to what is defined as masculine in America.

For Roth as for recent feminists gender identity is socially constructed. People are born biologically male or female, but they are not born masculine or feminine. They are trained to those gender identities by parents, teachers, siblings, and peers, not to mention TV, movies, teen magazines, advertising, and the world of fashion. To paraphrase Simone de Beauvoir, "One isn't born a man, one becomes one."[5] Thus "masculinity" and "femininity" may be succinctly defined as "patterns of sexuality and behavior imposed by cultural and social norms."[6] Like gender, ethnicity is also socially constructed. It is not, like skin or hair color or other distinguishing genetic features, inborn. As Michael J. Fischer recently put it, "Ethnicity is something reinvented and

WHAT DO MEN WANT, DR. ROTH?

reinterpreted in each generation by each individual, something puzzling, over which he or she lacks control. It is dynamic, not learned or passed from generation to generation."[7]

The nexus of ethnicity and gender—of Jewishness and masculinity—is central to Roth's work. It is clear that Roth's own relation to Jewishness is many-sided: "being Jewish" is for him an almost "tribal," "primitive," and arcane ethnicity.[8] Roth has commented that for him Jewishness is a question of style, the primarily verbal manifestation of that ethnic identity. And he noted recently, in answer to a question about the struggle with Jewishness in the Zuckerman trilogy, that

the Jewish quality of books like mine doesn't really reside in their subject matter. Talking about Jewishness hardly interests me at all. It's a kind of sensibility if anything: the nervousness, the excitability, the arguing, the dramatizing, the indignation, the obsessiveness, the touchiness, the play-acting, above all, the talking. It isn't what it's talking about that makes a book Jewish—it's that the book won't shut up. The book won't leave you alone. Won't let up. Gets too close. . . . I knew what I was doing when I broke Zuckerman's jaw. For a Jew a broken jaw is a terrible tragedy.[9]

Roth's emphasis on Jewishness as a given is, for the critic and essayist Alfred Kazin, one of the hallmarks of the second-generation Jewish writer. To Kazin, Saul

Bellow and Bernard Malamud are writers whose novels celebrate the Jewish situation, whereas Roth writes about "the self-conscious Jew, newly middle class," whose identity, "though established, is a problem to himself."[10] What Kazin means, in part, is that by the second generation Jews had successfully assimilated into the American mainstream, but they were not entirely comfortable there. For Roth, both personally and as a writer of fiction, his Jewishness is an essential condition. As Roth himself puts it, "I have always been far more pleased by my good fortune in being born a Jew than my critics may begin to imagine. It's a complicated, interesting, morally demanding, and very singular experience, and I like that. I find myself in the historic predicament of being Jewish, with all its implications."[11]

For Roth gender and ethnicity first come together explicitly in "The Jewboy" and "The Nice Jewish Boy," his early working drafts of *Portnoy's Complaint*. These terms delineate for him the limits and limitations of Jewish masculinity: "The 'Jewboy' (with all that word signifies to Jew and Gentile alike about aggression, appetite, and marginality) and the 'nice Jewish boy' (and what that epithet implies about repression, respectability, and social acceptance) . . . [were] the Abel and Cain of my own respectable middle-class background."[12] The "nice Jewish boy" and the "Jewboy" form the Dr. Jekyll and Mr. Hyde of Roth's as well as Portnoy's childhood. Obsessed with the conflict of Jewishness and masculin-

ity, Portnoy fights the battle between the Jewboy and
the nice Jewish boy, but *Portnoy's Complaint* reveals the
inadequacies of this polarization. Portnoy's desperation
leads to the questioning of the conventional relationship
between gender identity and ethnicity. At the same
time the novel reveals both the projective dynamic of
Jewishness and masculinity, and the damage it does to
the male and female characters (and real men and
women) who figure in it.

The action of *Portnoy's Complaint* is constructed as
a parody of the classic *Bildungsroman*. The hero's task,
in this male-centered genre, is to grow from the role of
the son into his "life as a man," to educate himself ethi-
cally and morally to take his rightful place in the world.
But the problem for Roth's protagonists in the novels
of his middle period is that though they, as good Jewish
sons, would seem to have had everything anybody
could want or need to grow up good and true, manhood
or full masculinity eludes them. And the novels suggest
that it is precisely because they are "good Jewish sons"
that the achievement of a straightforward masculinity
is the issue they must confront.

In *Portnoy's Complaint*, the earliest and most purely
comic of these middle novels, Alexander Portnoy deals
with his impotence and patent failure to "become a
man" by attempting a psychological interpretation.
What "makes men of . . . boys," or so Alex Portnoy
believes, is the capacity to "be bad—and enjoy it." In
other words, to grow up is to be able to stop being a

Jewish mother's well-behaved son and let the Jewboy in yourself go. Its objective correlative is Portnoy's rebellion against the laws of *kashrut*, both in his eager devouring of unkosher meat and lobster and his pursuit of non-Jewish women. But the "joke on Portnoy," Roth notes, is "that for him breaking the taboo turns out to be as unmanning in the end as honoring it."[13] Transgression, whether dietary or sexual, and its attendant guilt don't really get at the heart of Portnoy's complaint. What unmans Portnoy is his inability to choose between the conflicting claims of Jewishness (of either the Jewboy or the nice variety) and a more mainstream American masculinity.

In Alex Portnoy's version of his failures it is his family that keeps him from acquiring the grace and success of a quintessentially American mythological hero, his mother and father who keep him from becoming a Hemingway kind of man. Perhaps because his parents stand between him and American success, he becomes the Assistant Commissioner of Human Opportunity for New York City, seeking, in a position which is the epitome of the Jew as social worker who helps others acquire rights, that access to American privilege which consistently eludes him. For how, he complains, could Alex Portnoy grow up to be an American success with parents who demand at one and the same time academic achievement and strict kosher eating habits. The refrain he grows up with is Don't eat French fries after school, or hamburgers out. Alex includes their singsong

WHAT DO MEN WANT, DR. ROTH?

catalogue of dos and don'ts in his own voice—an index of the extent to which the voices of his parents have taken possession of him. " 'Hamburgers,' " his mother says bitterly,

just as she might say, *Hitler*, "where they can put any-thing in the world that they want—and *he* eats them. Jack, make him promise before he gives himself a terri-ble *tsura*, and it's too late."

"I *promise!*" I scream, "I *promise!*" and race from the kitchen—to where? Where else? (31).

Unable to assert his right to choose how and what he should eat, Alex Portnoy, would-be American individu-alist, rushes to the bathroom to claim his identity. He flees the ethnic boundaries of his mother's kitchen, whose taboos he cannot transgress, and hastens to the unlimited fantasy world of masturbation. The only weapon left him against their seduction of his inde-pendence is the signature act of his identity. Like a stand-up comic whose stock in trade is the transgres-sion of taboos, he one-ups them. He masturbates.

For Roth, kitchen and bathroom are fateful loca-tions. To take the kitchen and the bathroom seriously as places of human destiny puts the reader off balance and injects a nervous note into our reading, for food and fetishism are among the fundamental human taboos. The tension is released in the subsequent explosion of comedy: "I tear off my pants, furiously I grab that battered battering ram to freedom, my adolescent cock, even as my mother begins to call from the other side of the bathroom door. 'Now this time don't flush. Do you hear me, Alex? I have to see what's in that bowl!'" (32). His mother's pursuit of Alex's digestive processes makes him once more into a dependent child, but for the reader the scene is comic. She wants to see his bowel movements, while he asserts to Spielvogel, and by extension to the reader, that he's using the bathroom not for the excretion of kosher or unkosher food but to exercise his "battered battering ram to freedom" in an act of liberation. The comedy depends upon visualizing the dual perspectives, separated only by a door, on the same bathroom scene, one an adult's, the other a child's.

Ironically, Portnoy's insistence on justifying his own view leads inevitably and unconsciously to an understanding of his parents' fears. He begins his complaint with, "Doctor, do you understand what I was up against? My wang was all I really had that I could call my own." His words lead him to describe the obsessive parental supervision of his behavior which is all, as his mother sees it, that stands between him and the plague of the 1950s, polio.

You should have watched her at work during polio season! She should have gotten medals from the March of Dimes! "Open your mouth. Why is your throat red? Do

WHAT DO MEN WANT, DR. ROTH?

you have a headache you're not telling me about? You're not going to any baseball game, Alex, until I see you move your neck. Is your neck stiff? Then why are you moving it that way? You ate like you were nauseous, are you nauseous? Well, you ate like you were nauseous. I don't want you drinking from the drinking fountain in that playground. If you're thirsty wait until you're home. Your throat is sore, isn't it? I can tell how you're swallowing. I think maybe what you are going to do, Mr. Joe Di Maggio, is put that glove away and lie down. I am not going to allow you to go outside in this heat and run around, not with that sore throat, I'm not" (32).

Alex's monologue goes on to include his father's justification of their behavior. "Do you know why your mother when we go to the Chink's will never sit facing the kitchen?" Then his mother takes over this voicing of the demands of the superego: "Because I don't want to see what goes on back there. Alex, you must wash everything, is that clear? Everything! God only knows who touched it before you did" (33). The nagging tone and the obsessive insistence on cleanliness and hygiene reveal the single-mindedness of their middle-class Jewish hobbyhorse. The stuff of which comedy is made, this passage can also be read as revealing the inner social terror of the immigrant family that does not know how to read the cues of the larger society and so blankets everything different from what they themselves do with the same remark which is implicitly a prohibition: "That's *goyish*."

Alex Portnoy elicits the reader's sympathy because he has no chance to break away. His parents make it impossible for him to grow up. So long as these voices ring in his head, he cannot become an autonomous individual. He is unable to put aside his obsessive concentration on preadolescent and infantile behavior patterns. Though thirty at the time of this telling of his story, in his mother's eyes he is not yet toilet trained. For his parents none of the boundaries that separate adolescent behavior from adult conduct exist insofar as their darling Alex is concerned. Because their son is the hope of the immigrant—where they failed, he will succeed—they literally live in and through him, their voices informing every aspect of his life. As a result, Alex Portnoy's dream of individuality—the desire to be Joe DiMaggio—is undermined by the political realities of his American life, in which his family and community are dependent upon him for their success. The American dream cannot be his alone; his success must be for his family, clan, and people.

Though he is an adult in years, Alex's sexual patterns remain adolescent. As a child he countered the demands from the tribal kitchen by fleeing from them into the bathroom. Now he runs to and hides in the arms of Gentile women. His repudiation of the communal values his parents expect him to bring to successful fruition in America would be complete were he able to manage a successful adult relation with these non-Jewish women. But his failure to establish such a relationship reveals the depth of his unconscious commitment to those values he seemingly wants to abandon. Do what he may, the voices of his parents dominate his consciousness. He cannot evade the social responsibility instilled by his parents, and merely accept the taboos. "Who cares what I do, right, with what woman?" his defensive tone reveals how much he is repressing; the reader knows that everyone in his family is obsessed with what Alex Portnoy does, and with what woman.

The comedy of Portnoy's guilt at his violation of Jewish standards of cleanliness and the rules of *kashrut* as well as his obsessive masturbation, which as we have seen are linked, lead him to the discovery of guilt deeper and deeper within his personality. Since the traditional food rules of Jewish life forbid the mixing of milk and meat, "I couldn't even contemplate drinking a glass of milk with my salami sandwich without giving serious offense to God Almighty." There can be neither absolution nor escape. "Imagine then what my conscience gave me for all that jerking off! The guilt, the fears—the terror bred into my bones! What in their world was not charged with danger, dripping with germs, fraught with peril? Oh, where was the gusto, where was the boldness and courage?" (33). Portnoy's effort to grow up and move out of the house—to leave the safety of small-town New Jersey of the 1950s for the adventure of big-city life in the New York of endless possibility—becomes one of the basic expressions of his disagreement with his parents.

What Portnoy does not recognize is that the cause of his neurosis is not just a psychology of guilt but a guilt-inducing politics of fear and anxiety. For the world his mother fears is that urban, American, non-middle-class realm, where life is nasty, brutish, and short, and the war of all against all, whether bacteria, viruses, or the *goyim*, is unending. Portnoy's question—"Who filled these parents of mine with such fearful sense of life?"—has a plethora of appropriate answers. The paranoia of his parents has a basis in everyday life, as the survivors of this brutal century know full well. In the face of the awful possibilities his parents equate and make him confront as if they were equivalent plagues—polio, urban crime, high rents, and the Nazi production of mass death which always lurks in the consciousness of Roth's characters—they cannot simply reaffirm the values or the boundaries of ordinary middle-class life. For his parents as for Portnoy, and perhaps for his readers as well, life is indeed a tall tale in all its gruesomeness, monstrosity, and catastrophic absurdity. And this monologue of kitchen, bathroom, and bedroom is an attempt to sort out the possibilities that remain, in the hope of liberation.

In Alex's version of the failed "family romance" it is not simply that his mother is domineering and a nag, obsessive, and potentially castrating—she holds a knife over the six-year-old Alex because he will not eat—but that his father, his masculine role model, has already buckled under to the power of his mother.

If my father had only been my mother! and my mother my father! But what a mix-up of the sexes in our house! Who should by rights be advancing on me, retreating— and who should be retreating, advancing! Who should be scolding, collapsing in helplessness, enfeebled totally by a tender heart! And who should be collapsing, instead scolding, correcting, reproving, criticizing, faultfinding without end! Filling the patriarchal vacuum! (40).

But what does Alex mean by "should"? According to Barry Gross,[14] Alex derives his notions of proper American gender identity from the radio shows blaring throughout the Portnoy dinner hour. There the "fathers are men with . . . deep voices who never use double negatives" like "Jack Armstrong, the All-American Goy!" Their sons "know how to take motors apart" and aren't "afraid of anything physical" (144–45). Thus the difficulty for Alex lies in the conflicting messages he gets about masculinity from his Jewish-American home. Training him to be a perfect "little gentleman" this Jewish home is, he claims, preparing him for homosexuality rather than heterosexual masculinity. Indeed, Alex goes so far as to suggest that his pursuit of *shikses* has less to do with Gentile women as forbidden, or with himself as an appetitive Jewboy than it does with the idea that possessing a *shikse* will make him more like the *shkotzim*—their brothers, those "engaging, good-natured, confident, clean, swift, and powerful halfbacks for the college football teams" (144). Ultimately he concludes that sex with "nice" Gentile women like his college girlfriend Kay Campbell, whom he tellingly calls "The Pumpkin," or Sarah Abbott Maulsby, whom he even more baldly calls "The Pilgrim," is a means for him of appropriating their Americanness—"as though through fucking I will discover America. *Conquer* America" (235). In these terms, to be truly American is to reject one's ethnicity and its more fluid gender possibilities in favor of assimilation and its more rigid conception of American maleness. But Alex's resentment at what assimilation entails and his hostility toward the dominant culture are evidenced in his italicized emphasis on conquering and dominion.

Doth Alex protest too much? Despite his sexual and monologic acrobatics, Alex is not able to become a Jewish Joe DiMaggio and possess his own Marilyn Monroe. He cannot free himself of his parents' values and beliefs, and remains throughout very much his parents' son. And while that has proven emasculating, the American alternative doesn't really appeal to him either.

All they [Gentile men] know, these imbecilic eaters of the execrable, is to swagger, to insult, to sneer, and sooner or later to hit. . . . Also they know how to go out into the woods with a gun, these geniuses, and kill innocent wild deer. . . . Stupid *goyim!* Reeking of beer . . . home [they] head, a dead animal (formerly *alive*) strapped to each fender, so that all the motorists along the way can see how strong and manly [they] are (80).

Alex shares this view of masculinity in American culture from the 1950s through the 1970s with many women and some men. Nevertheless, for Alex abandoning what the dominant culture defines as masculine is as devastating for himself, his relationships with women, and those women themselves as his need to get out from under the Jewishness which has nourished these alternative values in the first place. Demasculated in the American (male) realm, he tries to reconstruct his masculinity by lording it over those whom he can dominate, American women, or, if you will, *shikses.*

Still, Alex is more his parents' son than he recognizes. The ironic connection between Alex's diminution by his parents' words and his efforts at escape through the *oral* domination of American, non-Jewish women will not escape the careful reader. He either seduces these women with his monologues, tells them insistently and obsessively how to behave sexually, or fixates on oral sexual maneuvers. The pattern is set in his childhood encounter with Bubbles Girardi. It continues to his relationship with Kay Campbell and Sarah Maulsby, and determines how he feels about Mary Jane Reed, nicknamed the Monkey for her sexual acrobatics.

Alex tries to overcome his shame at the sexual pleasure he has with these women, especially the Monkey, by seeking to improve them.

Try as he might, Alex cannot rid himself of his parents' values and words. Yet the memory of Ronald Nimkin's suicide haunts him and keeps urging him on to try. Ronald is the very model of the nice Jewish boy. Even when driven to suicide by his inability to live up to the expectations of this role, his last act is characteristic:

The detail of Ronald Nimkin's suicide that most appeals to me is the note to his mother found pinned to that roomy straitjacket, his nice, stiffly laundered sports shirt. Know what it said? Guess. The last message from Ronald to his momma? Guess.

Mrs. Blumenthal called. Please bring your mah-jongg rules to the game tonight. Ronald (119).

For Alex, the suicide epitomizes his own predicament. Why did Ronald Nimkin "give up his ghost and the piano?" Alex tells Dr. Spielvogel, imagining he is saying it to his mother: "BECAUSE WE CAN'T TAKE ANY MORE! BECAUSE YOU FUCKING JEWISH MOTHERS ARE JUST TOO FUCKING MUCH TO BEAR! . . . What do we want, me and Ronald? . . . *To be left alone!*" (120–21).

Against this figure of the nice Jewish boy Alex places that of his cousin Heshie, whom he admires. Heshie played football in high school and was engaged

WHAT DO MEN WANT, DR. ROTH?

to marry a non-Jewish baton twirler. After his parents paid her not to marry him, Heshie enlisted in the Marines to spite them, and was killed in the Korean war. This result, finally, is hardly better than Ronald Nimkin's and makes Alex wary of Heshie's alternative. Nevertheless, Alex cannot help but contrast his guilt with the feelings of his friends, who apparently feel no remorse in their sexual encounters. Smolka, the tailor's son, who lives on "Hostess cupcakes and his own wits," has advantages when it comes to sexual daring that Alex, who gets a "hot lunch and all the inhibitions thereof" does not (172). And Mandel, another high school buddy, does not use a condom during sexual intercourse, while Alex makes a fetish of them, filling them with water and playing with them continuously as a substitute for sexual interaction. They become his talismans, protecting him against venereal disease, of which he is terrified, and fathering children, which seems to him a terrible thing to do.

Alex pursues sexual fulfillment with non-Jewish women as a way of escaping from his Jewish mother, but because he never really does or can escape, he is driven to ever greater sexual extremes. In Rome he hires a prostitute to make a threesome with himself and the Monkey. The Monkey sees more clearly than Alex that this encounter degrades all three and breaks with him. This climax of the novel drives Alex to seek normal sexual fulfillment in Israel, the Jewish state. But in Israel, where Jews are not only professors and accountants but

UNDERSTANDING PHILIP ROTH

also drive taxicabs, defend their country, and do manual labor, Portnoy is a failure. He cannot seduce Naomi, the Sabra kibbutz member, who, it is no coincidence, resembles his mother. When she lectures him on his Jewish self-hatred, he listens without being convinced, though her confidence arouses him sexually. Trying in reaction to assert himself physically and rape her, he discovers she has been trained in the Israeli army to fight back. When she does agree to sexual intercourse, Alex cannot manage an erection. In the Zionist land where Jews are normal, Alex is an outsider and cannot function.

What is important about Alex's portrayal is not only the fundamental conflict between ethnicity and assimilation, but the ways in which Roth inscribes the traces of that determining conflict in Alex's struggle to define and express his manhood and social identity. How can Portnoy stop hating himself—by taking the "talking cure?" But he is already a masterful talker. What then is Portnoy's complaint? For Spielvogel, it is a new category of the "puzzled penis" problem. Alex's impotence, which is what has driven him to Dr. Spielvogel's couch to make his complaint in the first place, derives from the impossibility of either reconciling, or abdicating from, the conflicting claims of his Jewishness and American masculinity. But realizing this is no solution, nor is projecting his insecurity all over the place, whether by spewing his sperm everywhere or babbling endlessly about sex. But as any good therapist knows, talking

WHAT DO MEN WANT, DR. ROTH?

about it at least brings the problem into the open. Thus the only response Spielvogel can make to Portnoy's complaint is the novel's open-ended last line, "Now vee may perhaps to begin."

Focusing on the taboos of 1950s American life, highlighting the relationship between Alex's confusion and the destructive effect of his displaced anxiety on women, *Portnoy's Complaint* takes on an important cultural and political dimension. Roth claims as much for this novel in an important passage in his comments on his own work:

I sometimes think of my generation of men as the first wave of determined D-Day invaders, over whose bloody, wounded carcasses the flower children subsequently stepped ashore to advance triumphantly toward that libidinous Paris we had dreamed of liberating as we inched inland on our bellies, firing into the dark. "Daddy," the youngsters asked, "what did you do in the war?" I humbly submit they could do worse than read *Portnoy's Complaint* to find out.[15]

Thereby Roth aligns this novel of obsessive talk and masturbation with the liberating events of the American cultural revolution of the 1960s and 1970s.

Notes

1. Theodore Solotaroff, "Philip Roth: A Personal View," *Critical Essays on Philip Roth*, ed. Sanford Pinsker (Boston: Hall, 1982) 146.

2. Roth, *Reading Myself and Others* (New York: Farrar, Straus, 1975) 22.

3. Roth, *Portnoy's Complaint* (New York: Random House, 1969) 35. Further references will be noted parenthetically.

4. See Bernard F. Rodgers, Jr., *Philip Roth* (Boston: Twayne, 1978), especially 78–79; 115–118; 136–137.

5. *The Second Sex*, trans. H. M. Parshley, (New York: Knopf, 1953), ch. 1.

6. Toril Moi, *Sexual/Textual Politics* (New York: Methuen 1986) 65. At the same moment that gender studies has become a field of academic concern, ethnicity or ethnic studies has also moved inside the academy. In both cases marginalized groups, most notably women and some ethnic minorities, have forced a reevaluation of the way the world has been conventionally conceived, offering instead a more fluid, pluralistic perspective.

7. Michael J. Fischer, "Ethnicity and the Postmodern Arts of Memory," *Writing Culture*, ed. George Marcus and James E. Clifford (Berkeley: University of California Press, 1986) 195.

8. Mark Schechner, "Philip Roth," Pinsker 123.

9. Interview with Philip Roth by Asher Z. Milbauer and Donald G. Watson, *Reading Philip Roth* (New York: St. Martin's Press, 1988); excerpted in *The New York Times Book Review* 4 Jan. 1987: 24.

10. Alfred Kazin, "The Earthly City of the Jews," Pinsker 106.

11. *Reading Myself and Others* 20.

12. *Reading Myself and Others* 35, 37.

13. *Reading Myself and Others* 19.

14. Barry Gross, "Sophie Portnoy and 'The Opossum's Death': American Sexism and Jewish Anti-Gentilism," *Studies in American Jewish Literature* 3 (Albany: State University of New York Press, 1983), 166–78.

15. *Reading Myself and Others* 8.

CHAPTER FIVE

American Rites: *Our Gang* (1971); *The Breast* (1972); *The Great American Novel* (1973)

Our Gang

Two years after the worldwide success of *Portnoy's Complaint* and its sexual comedy, Roth turned to political satire. *Our Gang* extended the range of his fictional universe. As its title indicates, the object of his attack is not just one person but a group, and the gang he satirizes enacts in Roth's view the absurd values of the Vietnam era. The novel is cast in the form of a play with the character parts identified in capital letters on the left. The format indicates that everyone is playing a preordained role; it also underlines the fact that Roth expects the reader to recognize the actual people his characters represent. His satire as well marks the era in which it takes place by including actual figures such as Curt Flood and Lieutenant Calley.

Our Gang is a contemporary Swiftian satire. In the course of its six brief chapters of social and political commentary the President of the United States, Tricky E. Dixon, talks his way from seeming rationality to absurdity, and ends up convicting himself in his own words. What at the beginning of this tale seems to be willful self-deception is at the end exposed as deliberate lying. This theme is established in the novel's two epigraphs. The first is a comment on deception and the universal human "Faculty of Lying," from "A Voyage to the Houhnyhms," the fourth book of Swift's *Gulliver's Travels*. The second epigraph, about the decay of language and the use of political language "to make lies sound truthful and murder respectable," is taken from George Orwell's essay "Politics and the English Language." Roth brackets the text of his novel between quotations, concluding with a quote from the Book of Revelation in which the angel casts the devil into the pit and seals it "that he should deceive the nations no more."

The satire of the use of political language is part of the polemic purpose of the book which, published in 1971, was directed at President Nixon, who was preparing his campaign for reelection. Roth's concern with the ways in which deception and political lying turn every citizen into a self-deceiver is carried forward into the analysis of the disruption of American English by political corruption. In this way he responds to Orwell's call to improve the "present political chaos" by making words correspond more closely to things.

On the page facing the beginning of chapter 1 Roth quotes President Nixon's views on the unacceptability of abortion. As the first chapter begins, Tricky responds to a citizen troubled by abortion in phrases that echo the quote. Tricky E. Dixon moves quickly from his defense of the "sanctity of human life" to a defense of Lieutenant Calley, the murderer of twenty-two Vietnamese civilians at My Lai. The exchange between Tricky and the citizen moves from detail to detail in such a way that Tricky can connect them all to his conscience and "refusal to do the popular thing."[1] The citizen, whose mind is as slippery as Tricky's, is troubled that perhaps one of the women killed by Calley was pregnant, and in that case an abortion would have been performed. Tricky points out that while there were babies in the ditch, there were no pregnant women. Yet even if there were, Calley had no way of knowing a particular woman was not just stout but actually carrying a child. Consequently Tricky, the lawyer, notes that Calley cannot be charged with providing abortion on demand. Calley therefore cannot be guilty. By this exchange the actual charge for which Calley was convicted is obfuscated. Furthermore, Roth deftly underscores the irony of condemning abortion while condoning the wholesale murder of innocent Vietnamese peasants, thereby pointing to the absurdities of this moment in American politics. Tricky concludes the chapter with a delicious example of slippery language: "'And if . . . I should find in the evidence against the lieutenant anything whatsoever that I cannot square with my personal belief in the sanctity of human life, including the life of the yet unborn,'" he states, leading up to what should by its legal logic conclude with a statement of Calley's guilt. Instead, the sentence ends with an unexpected and yet seemingly straightforward conclusion: "I will disqualify myself as a judge and pass the entire matter on to the Vice President" (10). Though illogical, this statement is rhetorically persuasive.

The second chapter takes the form of a mock presidential news conference. Tricky Dixon speaks out for the granting of the vote to the yet unborn, which, he reluctantly admits, will provide him with a wave of friendly voters and assure him of reelection. In this way Tricky will be "to the unborn" what "Martin Luther King was to the black people of America and the late Robert F. Charisma to the disadvantaged chicanos and Puerto Ricans of the country" (11). Of course, this new group is larger than any ethnic group, and their votes will sweep Tricky into a second term. When asked how the unborn will go about casting their ballots, since they have no developed nervous system or limbs, Tricky reminds his listeners that handicapped people have the right to vote. Of course, they don't make news the way demonstrators, do, he insists. When asked about the innocence of fetuses, Tricky responds that their innocence is just what the country needs. "'We've had the foul language, we've had the cynicism, we've had the masochism and the breast-beating—maybe a big dose of innocence is just what this country needs to be great again'" (22).

The novel moves to the crisis of the third chapter

when Dixon discovers that his advocacy of rights for the unborn has been taken as evidence by the Boy Scouts that he is in favor of sexual intercourse. Tricky weathers the crisis with the help of his aides, who discuss the entire problem in the presidential "blastproof underground locker room," dressed in football uniforms. In fact, whenever he faces difficulties, Tricky "suits up" and plays an imaginary game of football to calm himself.

And invariably, as during the Cambodian incursion and the Kent State killings, simply to don shoulder guards, cleats, and helmet, to draw the snug football pants up over his leather athletic supporter and then to turn his back to the mirror and catch a peek over his big shoulders at the number on his back, is enough to restore his faith in the course of action he has taken in behalf of two hundred million Americans (25–26).

The football uniform restores Tricky's sense of his own power. President Nixon's well-known love of professional football thus becomes a central device in Roth's satire. This image of the President playing dress-up emphasizes both the macho and the childish values at work here. The parody reveals the adolescent qualities legitimated by the American culture of sports. Dixon's discussion with his aides of how he might dissociate himself from the charge of advocating fornication leads to some hilarious exchanges, including one where

Dixon and his staff consider that he announce on national television that not only has he never engaged in fornication himself (his children are adopted, he will tell everyone), but he is in fact a homosexual. This scheme crumbles when he is informed by one of his staff, his SPIRITUAL COACH, that homosexuals also engage in intercourse. Having previously agreed not to let his MILITARY COACH order the shooting of the demonstrating Boy Scouts, Tricky finally agrees to the suggestion made by his HIGHBROW COACH that they find someone to blame for this disruption of the social order.

The advisers make lists and settle on Curt Flood as their scapegoat. In 1968 the real Curt Flood, a remarkable black athlete who played center field for the St. Louis Cardinals, refused to be traded to the Philadelphia Phillies, challenging the reserve clause that at the time was standard in all professional baseball contracts.[2] Tricky has the Commissioner of Baseball accuse Curt Flood on national television of actions that "would destroy the game of baseball as we know it" (95). According to Tricky, Flood is one of the principal agitators disrupting the social order in the era of the Vietnam and Cambodian wars, and the leader of the antiwar demonstrations in Washington. President Tricky E. Dixon then accuses Flood of fleeing the country "on April 27, 1971, exactly one week to the day before the uprising of the Boy Scouts in Washington" (94). The fact that Curt Flood is black inclines people, Tricky suggests, to understand that he is capable of terrible things, among them the subversion of the morals and values of even so patriotic a group as the Boy Scouts of America. The ironies here are multiple, from parallels between baseball and America, which Roth develops further in *The Great American Novel*, to the implication that Flood's refusal to be traded to the Philadelphia Phillies baseball team, rather than the actions of the government, caused political unrest and antiwar demonstrations. In Roth's fiction Flood becomes a political touchstone: an example of true American heroism opposing the power of the dominant system. He stands with Roth's other folk heroes from minority groups, such as Sacco and Vanzetti, anarchists convicted of armed robbery on circumstantial evidence and executed in 1927 during a Red scare. Roth also associates Flood with Ethel and Julius Rosenberg, children of immigrant Jews who were convicted of espionage and executed in 1953 on the charge of passing nuclear weapons secrets to the Soviet Union in an era of political hysteria and rabid anticommunism.

In the fourth chapter Dixon addresses the nation to persuade them that it is necessary to bomb Denmark, which has given refuge to Curt Flood, the alleged instigator of the current wave of social unrest. Dixon reminds his people that Denmark is the capital of pornography and this is further evidence that it must be destroyed. And just to add a literary twist, the title of the "Famous 'Something is Rotten in the State of Denmark' Speech," parodies Hamlet's line, as well as echoing some notable political speeches of Nixon's. Furthermore, Dixon presents the attack on Denmark as an exact replay of what his predecessor, "John F. Charisma," did in preventing Soviet nuclear missiles from entering Cuba and the Western Hemisphere. Tricky's reference is to John F. Kennedy's daring confrontation with Nikita Khruschev and Fidel Castro during the Cuban missile crisis, though he does not mention the subsequent debacle of the Bay of Pigs invasion of 1961. Dixon further casts anti-Semitic and antiliberal aspersions on his scapegoat by emphasizing that Flood's legal counsel is Arthur Goldberg, a Jew and former Supreme Court Justice.

The fifth chapter, "The Assassination of Tricky," reveals how language, which Dixon has worked so assiduously to undermine, has become a net in which he is entangled. The vice-president leads the cascade of nonsense which concludes with a page of "Blah blah blah." Finally, the sixth chapter takes the form of a campaign speech by Tricky for the job of leading the forces of Hell. The political impact of *Our Gang*, and by extension American involvement in Southeast Asia, comes to a head in Dixon's statement that his record as President of the United States qualifies him, more than Satan, for the job of chief devil. "I think you will agree that in the very brief time allotted to me I managed to seize upon the opportunity . . . and, with the aid of the United States Air Force, I turned [Southeast Asia] into nothing less than Hell on earth" (193). Tricky concludes his speech with the traditional political flourish of the campaigner—now, however, free of the deceptions he has always previously practiced to obscure his real goals. "And let there be no mistake about it: if I am elected Devil, I intend to see Evil triumph in the end; I intend to see that our children, and our children's children, need never know the terrible scourge of Righteousness and Peace" (200).

Roth's dramatic enactment of the political uses and abuses of language unmasks the process by which these Americans seek scapegoats for their failures, and condemns the corrupt and corrupting tactics of those holding even the country's most sacrosanct offices. The attacks on Curt Flood, Arthur Goldberg, the Boy Scouts, the student anti-Vietnam demonstrators, and Planned Parenthood all serve to mask the costs of an unjust war and, in Roth's views, regressive social values. He adopts the classic tactic of satire, whereby his characters convict themselves with the words that come out of their own mouths.

The Breast

The Breast, a brief retrospective narrative told in a first-person monologue, is David Kepesh's attempt to account for the process that has transformed him into a giant breast. His identity as a Jew, as an American, and as a man is, as is the case with many other Roth heroes, problematic. He is constantly trying to sort out who and what, exactly, he is, in this ironic tale of what it means to be a professor of desire—the title of Roth's later novel in which Kepesh is also the main character.

Kepesh begins his tale with musings upon the "odd" events of life, whereby a slight tingling in the groin leads in twenty-one days to a pinkish stain he first thinks is cancer. That night, alarmed by the pigment change, he telephones his physician, who offers to see him immediately, but Kepesh tells himself to take hold of the situation, and they set a meeting time for nine the next morning. As he relives the unfolding events of that fateful night of transformation, Kepesh meditates upon his relationship with Claire Ovington. Over the three years of their relationship they have worked out a way of being together while living apart to maintain their independence. He believes that it has kept them from the inevitable difficulties—the grinding boredom, dependence, unfocused yearning, deception, and dominance—of married life. But their decision to live separately as individuals rather than entering the joined condition of marriage has kept them isolated, insulating them in their individualism. It has also left Kepesh to face his transformation alone.

The Breast is a troubling tale. Like Kafka's "Metamorphosis" and Gogol's "The Nose," both of which it self-consciously echoes and refers to, Roth's narrative is full of misleading interpretive possibilities that must be sorted out. Much of Kepesh's time is devoted to trying to figure out what his transformation means. As each possibility is ruled out, Kepesh is left to reflect anew upon his transformed shape. It is possible to argue that this tale is an allegory of interpretation. It is also possible to argue that *The Breast* is a straightforward tale of mythical transformation, which focuses on the comedy of male pride, for no matter what happens, David Kepesh cannot relinquish his male ego. As the narrative unfolds, the breast he has turned into accumulates, rather than reflects, projects, introjects, or represents meanings in allegorical or symbolic ways. Kepesh's transformation is not explained by any or all of them. The genetic explanation is as useless as the allegorical or the symbolic one. Over and over again Kepesh confronts the opaqueness of meaning of his breastly form, hoping it will help him account for his weird state by yielding a narrative. Kepesh concludes the first chapter by noting that what has happened to him seems to have no scientific explanation. His comment invokes mythic situations, like that in which the Greek seer Tiresias was transformed into a woman in order to solve the ancient riddle as to whether men or women feel greater pleasure in sexual intercourse. Playing with modern biology to achieve a parallel effect, Roth creates a contemporary fable that explores the links among female sexuality, male individualism, and the power of thought to define and maintain a sense of personal identity.

In the second chapter Kepesh describes his new condition. Between midnight and four A.M. on February 18, 1971, an unexplained event—a freakish hormonal imbalance or explosion of chromosomes—converted him into a huge "mammary gland" unconnected to any human form. He can no longer see himself but can hear and speak through the rosy aureole around his nipple. He is informed by his physician that he is in a private room on the seventh floor of Lenox Hill Hospital in New York City, suspended in a hammock. Nurses attend him. When they oil his nipple, he finds the sexual pleasure excruciating, though eventually he is able to bear washing. He does not know whether to believe that he is in a hospital or on display in a department store window. He is visited by various doctors, including his psychoanalyst, Dr. Klinger, and discovers that he is able to think with great clarity. In fact, it is impossible for him to go mad and lose himself despite his desire to do so. He is obsessed by questions of identity and has no desire to die, insisting, like Gregor Samsa of Kafka's "Metamorphosis," that despite his change he yet remains human. With Dr. Klinger's help he begins to meditate on the ordinary events of life.

Chapter 3 centers on an account of his visitors, who include his father, Claire, and his psychoanalyst. David dwells on his father's life as a hotelkeeper in South Fallsburg, New York. He appreciates the stories his father tells him of old friends and admires his father's ability to keep up the performance.

AMERICAN RITES

When Claire comes to see him and rests her head upon him, pangs of self-doubt assail him. He wonders if he would have been able to continue to love her had she turned into a penis. This leads him to realize that despite his altered state he has not been able to change his way of assessing his self-worth. Even now he constantly compares himself to others, even though he knows that comparisons are odious. He criticizes himself for his deficiencies and insensitivities but also praises himself for his positive qualities, believing that he is now practicing the virtue of modesty. Ironically, the passivity his shape enforces makes him aware of the power of male sexuality just at the moment when he has taken on female characteristics. He begins to muse about his mother, who is dead. Claire's presence in his hospital room makes him reflect upon their habits as lovers. The night of his transformation Claire was staying in her apartment completing a committee report while Kepesh, alone, was musing about his waning passion for Claire, which had led him to seek therapeutic help.

One result of his transformation, however, has been to make Kepesh dependent upon her. His changed condition has made him both more susceptible to sensual delight than ever before and more demanding. Kepesh believes they have always been passionate, but not unusual lovers. Now he registers his surprise in realizing his intense need for forms of pleasure he has associated more with women than men. Claire's willingness to give him pleasure by sucking his nipple, now five inches long, yields excruciating delight, reminding him of their early sexual encounters. But the sudden intensity of his new feelings makes him apprehensive. In his new condition he is all feeling, his earlier problem of lessening passion having been taken care of by his transformation.

With time on his hands Kepesh muses about the new intensities of his condition, acknowledging his homophobia for the first time. He admits he desperately wants Claire's companionship, and since his sexual excitement cannot be released but remains constantly at the same high level of intensity, he is even willing to limit it for the chance to have her visit on a regular basis. Fearful that his sexual frenzy will drive Claire away, David makes increasingly lewd suggestions to the nurses. Instead of having to talk about his waning passion with his psychoanalyst he now must discuss his overwhelming lust.

David's former department chairman, now the Dean of the College of Arts and Sciences at Stony Brook, visits him in the next chapter. Arthur Schonbrunn is a suave academic politician, who has brought David from Stanford to teach at Stony Brook. When he sees David in his new condition, Arthur Schonbrunn giggles. Though he tries to suppress it, he cannot control his laughter at the sight of his former colleague now transformed into a gigantic beast. Two weeks later Arthur apologizes and sends David the Laurence Olivier re-

AMERICAN RITES

cording of *Hamlet*. This launches David into listening to all of Shakespeare's plays and learning all the parts.

The shock of Arthur's visit convinces David the entire transformation is psychosomatic. David is convinced that he is suffering from a delusion, and tells Dr. Klinger it is caused by the books he has been teaching in his European Literature course, especially Gogol's "The Nose" and Kafka's "Metamorphosis." Unlike others who teach these books, David claims to teach them with devoted conviction; now he has convinced himself he has gone mad. Klinger assures him, however, that he is perfectly sane and has undergone a physiological rather than a psychic transformation. David will not believe him. He tells his father that he is overcoming his delusions and will soon return to teaching Gogol and Kafka rather than experiencing the transformations they had imagined in their books. His father has not read them, and so in his more rational moments, acting once more as a teacher of literature, David summarizes these great works for him. When he stops babbling about his delusion, his father tells David that he is in fact a breast. Yet he humors David and agrees that he is a mental patient. Ultimately David is forced to accept the fact of his transformation.

In the last chapter David has found a daily routine, which includes listening to Shakespeare, talking with Claire and his father, and reflecting upon the strangeness of the human condition. Kepesh now slips into his old habit as a teacher of literature and delivers lectures, even when talking about himself. His formal words make his transformation into a literary event: he has become a text for interpretation. The strange event that has occurred becomes a lesson. Though his monologue is full of ironic reflections, by its close he thinks of himself objectively, and concludes by drawing a general moral. "Morons and madmen, tough guys and skeptics, friends, students, relatives, colleagues . . . with your billion different fingerprints and faces . . . my fellow mammalians, let us proceed with our education, one and all."[3] Kepesh thus gives voice to the motto governing much of Roth's fiction: life is in fact a continuing process of adaptation, accommodation, and education.

But Kepesh has been devoted to this principle of education. At the end of the tale he is led to ask why he of all people has been singled out for this terrible transformation. As he casts about for an answer, Kepesh locates it in fiction. He has devoted himself to the teaching of literature with the passion of a religious calling. His transformation is the physical incarnation of his calling: as a professor of desire David Kepesh has achieved his literary apotheosis. That is how he justifies himself to Klinger: " 'After all,' I said, 'who is the greater artist, he who imagines the marvelous transformation, or he who marvelously transforms himself?' " The young man who embraced the literary works of Western culture with the devotion of the new believer has been transformed, he believes, into the incarnation of the values of the highest literary art. "Why David Kepesh? Why me, of all people, endowed with such powers? . . . Why anyone? Great art happens to people like anything else. And this is my great work of art!" But David Kepesh is too defensive and sophisticated to accept this as a straightforward answer. Hearing in his own words an echo of the self-delusion with which *Gulliver's Travels* ends, Kepesh quickly rolls to the other extreme: "'Ah,' but I quickly added, 'I must maintain my sane and reasonable perspective. I don't wish to upset you again. No delusions—delusions of grandeur least of all'" (480).

Like Portnoy's, Kepesh's imagination is endlessly fertile, tossing up possibility after possibility, none of which he excludes and all of which seem to him to express another side of his nature. What he cannot do is decide on one and give it priority. "*Did* fiction do this to me?" he asks himself.

"How could it have?" asks Dr. Klinger. "No, hormones are hormones and art is art. You are not suffering from an overdose of the great imaginations." "Aren't I? I wonder. This might well be my way of being a Kafka, being a Gogol, being a Swift. They could envision the incredible, they had the words and those relentless fictionizing brains. But I had neither, I had nothing—literary longings and that was it. I loved the extreme in literature, idolized those who wrote it, was virtually hypnotized by the imagery and the power—" (479–80).

"And? Yes?" Klinger asks.

Roth dramatizes the obsessiveness with which Kepesh reads great literature at the same time that he satirizes it, punctuating the heroic mood with Klinger's matter-of-factness.

Like a mother's breast, books have nourished the fantasies of this professor of literary desire. Now, in a striking inversion, he becomes an incarnation of the primal source of all human nourishment. In his imagination it is his literary fantasies—his professing of desire—that have caused this transformation. His monologue proposes that change and transformation are everywhere in human life. The narrative concludes with a direct address that emphasizes this view: "You must change your life," the concluding line of a famous poem by the German modernist poet Rainer Maria Rilke. Kepesh uses it to sum up the meaning of what has happened to him. Rather than the poem explaining his life, his life now illuminates the poem. He has not been satisfied just to teach literature or even to write it, but has become a living incarnation of modern literature itself. Kepesh, professor of desire, has become one with the books that he professed.

The Great American Novel

In *The Great American Novel*, Roth combines the sexual and psychological satire of *The Breast* and the political concerns of *Our Gang* to produce a parody of American life. The vehicle for the satire is baseball, America's national pastime. Roth begins with the assumption that baseball is in fact the civil religion of America. He takes the central experiences of baseball—skill and team play—and abstracts them into values, thus giving them an overly serious inflection. Then he pursues his hilarious equation of the intertwining of politics and sex with the practice of this game in which all red-blooded American males are covenanted believers. As one of the characters puts it, "For what is a ball park, but that place wherein Americans may gather to worship the beauty of God's earth, the skill and strength of His children, and the holiness of His commandment to order and obedience. For such are the twin rocks upon which all sport is founded."[4] The effect of the religious diction is not so much to elevate the American pastime as to make it an allegory of American life. The accents of this language echo those of Red Barber, the voice of the Brooklyn Dodgers. The difference between his soft, southern inflection with its elevated, even courtly diction, which he used to describe the antics of "dem bums," and the gritty reality of the baseball they in fact played defines the space in which this parodic fiction works. The first chapter concludes with Fairsmith, the Mundys manager, playing the role of Moses and asking the league to "let his players go." Each chapter from that point on interweaves baseball, contemporary politics, literary allusions, and echoes of biblical scenes to create a layered texture. The mythic overtones of the narrative are set by the epigraph to the novel, which defines the "great American novel" as a work not extinct like the dodo but rather, like the hippogriff, a mythical beast. Here parody and farce replace heroic American myth.

In the prologue Roth introduces a retired yet still crusading sports writer, ironically named Word Smith, who speaks directly to the reader. From his first words, which echo the "Call me Ishmael" with which *Moby-Dick* opens, Smith is out to persuade the reader of his sincerity and sanity. He also wants to make sure his linguistic abilities are appreciated. "Call me Smitty," Word Smith announces. "That's what everybody" calls him—"the ballplayers, the bankers, the bareback riders, the baritones, the bartenders, the bastards, the best-selling writers" (1). Roth's characteristic juxtaposition of the language of high culture and folk speech is central to the rhetorical strategy of *The Great American Novel*. Here Smitty's addiction to alliteration, dangerously out of control, takes the habit of most sports writers to its extreme. He concludes the first paragraph by calling attention, like a literary Howard Cosell, to his prowess: "'And that's only the letter B, fans, only *one* of the Big Twenty-Six!'" Furthermore, as a writer he has the virtues of an athlete, including the ability to perform his task brilliantly, and he does not hesitate to show off his linguistic talent. Like much else in the novel, however, this comes close to producing nonsense. Alliteration, he claims, saved his life when he was in the hospital. As if to pay off his debt Smitty is now engaged in saving the soul of baseball by recovering the memory of a baseball league that has been written out of history.

Word Smith's only weapon in his struggle is the play of language. Smitty loves to make catalogues of words and alliterative sequences, as if he were a contemporary Walt Whitman. Smith relies on his rich American English to serve as the bolstering memory of the past. Virtuoso of talk and baseball writer extraordinaire, Word Smith subjects his culture to a public equivalent of Portnoy's talking cure. Both patient and psychoanalyst, Word Smith, like Portnoy, seeks to heal a culture's wounds through a process of linguistic therapy. Roth thus defines the writer's task not only as that of bearing witness to the true shape of his culture's values, fears, and dreams, but as that of confronting the political decisions that define its shapes and possibilities in the first place. The corruption of baseball in the 1940s makes Word Smith desperate. Political corruption extends to language; Smitty shows his prowess by parodying his hero, Hemingway, as well as the classic works of nineteenth-century American literature, *The Scarlet Letter*, *Adventures of Huckleberry Finn*, and *Moby-Dick*.

As a journalist Smith connects the world of sports and writing. He too is fascinated by the idea of the great American novel, a subject he has raised, he tells us, with Hemingway on his fishing boat. The episode is a parody both of Hemingway's habit of entertaining his friends on his boat and of his novel *The Old Man and the Sea*, published just before he received the Nobel Prize for Literature in 1954. Roth's parody calls Hemingway's legendary all-American skill and sexual prowess into question. The reason for his behavior, Smitty suggests, is that Hemingway is fishing for the great American novel, which he claims requires the greatest courage, technical skill, and manliness to write. Neither modest nor reluctant to speak about his own virtues, Word Smith notes that he is the writer Hemingway expects will write the great American novel. But instead of the seriousness of literary discussions, their exchange sounds like self-advertisement. Writing is a macho persona and profession for Smitty, as for Hemingway. Discussions of values turn into questions of technique; these are "tough hombres" sorting out what really matters. It is no accident that Hem, which is the name Smitty gives him, calls all women "slits" to put them in their place. For Hem, the great American novel has no room for independent, assertive women.

Further on in the prologue Smitty launches into a long complaint against all those institutions that are trying to wipe out American memory, the true subject, he notes, of the greatest American novels and works of art. Therefore, he decides to write the untold story of the Patriot League and its bizarre teams—the Ruppert Mundys, Tri-City Tycoons, Terra Incognita Rustlers, Asylum Keepers, Kakoola Reapers, and Tri-City Greenbacks— all of whom he claims have been excluded from American sports history for political reasons. As an artist Smith finds himself standing against those political forces that want to sanitize American history. One of the major objects of Smith's wrath is Bowie Kuhn, the commissioner of major league baseball, who enforces the rules of the game and keeps the archives closed.

Roth casts a scornful eye on cherished American habits and values by taking them seriously and literally. Instead of reaffirming the values of home, mother, and apple pie, this "great American novel" of baseball—America's religion—ironically reveals how the players have been corrupted by recent American politics. Instead of making heroes out of baseball players, they become scapegoats for the failures of American culture. The first chapter, entitled "Home Sweet Home," tells the story of "why the Ruppert Mundys had been chosen to become the homeless team of baseball" (49). The key moment foreshadowing this grim event is the decision not to let the Mundys have a home stadium. After that, the Mundys are always on the road. In the second chapter, "The Visitors' Lineup," they become examples of an uprooted America that is always away from home. Though they have set records in all areas of baseball that would have made them the greatest team in the history of the game, they have been cast out from the history of baseball because of their political transgressions. The third chapter, "In the Wilderness," continues the story of the traveling Mundys, digresses to include a long episode about the Patriot Negro League, and concludes with the breakup of the champion Mundys. After that, they can only get cripples to play for them. Chapter 4, "Every Inch a Man," contains the entire history of the participation of midgets in professional baseball and plays on the only actual participation of a midget in the game, sponsored by Bill Veeck of the Chicago White Sox. The chapter then takes flight into the adventures of Bud Parusha, the one-armed outfielder.

At one point near the end of chapter 5 Isaac Ellis, a boy genius, devises an entirely new, brilliant strategy for the game of baseball (which might also be understood as an analogue for American art). This discovery brings the hope of success to the hapless Greenbacks, a haphazard collection of cripples and misfits. Isaac's father, the owner of the team, engages in an exchange with him that echoes the conversations between Portnoy and his father. " 'You're such a genius, do me a favor, prove dey're *right.*' 'But that's not what geniuses *do.*' 'I dun care about de oder geniuses! I only care about *you!*' " Then his father concludes the exchange by praising his country. "Only in America could a Jew ever hope to become the owner of a major league baseball team!" This paean of praise to America draws a political answer from the son. " 'Isaac—listen to me, for a Jewish pois'n dis is de greatest country vat ever vas, in de history of the *voild!*' 'Sure it is, Dad,' said the contemptuous son, 'as long as he plays the game their way' " (272). It is a comment that Roth intends to echo the fate of Curt Flood. Isaac's strategy is brilliant; the only trou-

AMERICAN RITES

ble is that it ruins the Greenbacks by forcing them to think about a game that until then had been a matter of unconscious reflexes. American art will now, like Hamlet, have to confront the paralyzing potential of thought.

In chapters 5 and 6, the great Mundy outfielder, Roland Agni, encounters the temptations of Jesus, now set in the modern context of American baseball in the late 1940s. Agni, the brilliant center fielder, must deal with the frustration of being the perfect baseball player on a team of misfits. His attempted seduction by the owner's mistress brings Agni to the logical conclusion of supreme sacrifice. The religious imagery and Christian allusions are continued as the manager of the Mundys, Fairsmith, takes baseball to Africa to civilize and thereby save the natives in a wicked parody of Joseph Conrad's *Heart of Darkness*, complete with a parodic bout of mock cannibalism in which the angered tribesmen eat not Fairsmith and his helper but all the baseball equipment.

Chapter 7, "The Return of Gil Gamesh; or, Mission from Moscow," reveals the extent of the infiltration of the international communist conspiracy into the Patriot League. It is this most un-American activity that causes the removal of the Patriot League from the collective memory of American life. As it turns out, all the members of the Ruppert Mundys are either actively involved in spying for the Soviet Union or duped into passing secrets to the enemy by hiding microfilm in hollow bats or secreting it in their jockstraps. Gil Gamesh, previously banished from the league for trying to kill Mike the Mouth Masterson, the umpire who had ruined his rookie season, returns as a double agent. Isaac Ellis now adds to his original baseball strategy; he feeds his players drugged Wheaties, which really do make them champions, thus fulfilling the cereal's motto as "the breakfast of champions." The absurdities of these situations central to *The Great American Novel* also echo those of *Our Gang;* Gil Gamesh, the double agent, invokes the double-dealing of Tricky E. Dixon, and the rhetorical double-talk and self-conscious allegory recall the political language of *Our Gang.*

The parodic qualities of *The Great American Novel* extend to its characters' names: Gil Gamesh is made from the name of the Babylonian epic hero, Gilgamesh, whose story echoes that of Noah's flood narrative; and Baal is the name of the major Canaanite god in the Hebrew Bible. The novel also echoes and parodies the emphasis in many biblical passages on the origin of traditions and customs (known as aetiological narratives). The prohibition against the use of the spitball is traced to the pitcher Baal, who in the 1902 World Series uses various substances including earwax to alter the flight of the baseball. As a result a rule is passed forbidding any player from anointing "the ball with any bodily secretions for any purpose whatsoever" (107). This rule so infuriates Baal, now pitching under the alias of Spit, that on the opening day of the 1903 season, when, after "throwing nothing but bone dry pitches, Spit is tagged for eight hits and five runs before he had anyone out in the first inning," he takes direct action. Taking his failure personally, blaming "those dryball bastards" who "had passed a law whose purpose was the destruction of no one in the world but himself," Spit did the "unthinkable, the unpardonable, the inexpiable." Dropping his uniform trousers, he urinated on the ball, "turning it slowly in his hands so as to dampen the entire surface," and, calling to the batter—"as frozen in his position as anyone else in the ball park"—yells to him, " 'Here comes the pissball, shithead.' " And the rest is the stuff of legend:

For years afterward they talked about the route that ball took before it passed over the plate. Not only did it make the hairpin turns and somersaults expected of a Baal spitter, but legend has it that it shifted gears *four* times, halving, then doubling its velocity each fifteen feet it traveled. And in the end, the catcher, in his squat, did not even have to move his glove from where it too was frozen as a target. Gagging, he caught the ball with a *squish*, right in the center of the strike zone (107–08).

Roth presents the scatological side of baseball—a game played not by adults, but by overgrown boys—as part of his allegorical method.

The catastrophic events of the baseball season that lead to the dissolution of the Patriot League reveal that baseball has ceased to be an activity played for its own sake and has become a business run for political reasons

by insidious corporations. Of course, the very name of
the league serves as part of the satire, for those who
present themselves as patriots in this world, like Tricky
E. Dixon, are actually the biggest scoundrels. The players are victimized by the owners; but when the players
become unruly and contemplate revolutionary action,
communism is blamed, and the entire Patriot League is
not only put out of business but its records are simply
expunged from history. Gil Gamesh implicates the pure
Roland Agni in his dastardly plot to pass microfilm to
the enemy. Agni becomes the fall guy; Gil Gamesh has
the heroic role. History is rewritten from the point of
view of the victor. Thus Roth makes the further point
that those who control the media of communication
shape the people's perception of events and, by extension, of history itself.

The epilogue consists of an exchange of letters between Word Smith and his readers, including a letter
Word writes Chairman Mao about the plight of the artist
in America. *The Great American Novel* concludes by undermining the assumptions on which the myth of the
heroic American artist/athlete is based. Like the Mundys, the American writer is encouraged to dream of
success as a hero, only to be brought up short and written out of history when the logic of his achievement
leads him to redefine his cultural role. At this point
Roth's satirical presentation of American history in the
form of a parody of the Bible, American literature, and
recent American politics doubles back upon his narra-

tor. Because of his overweening self-righteousness he makes everything fit the purposes of his own self-justification. Smitty's obsessiveness makes him monomaniacal: he has become the Ahab of American sports writing.

Notes

1. Roth, *Our Gang* (New York: Random House, 1971) 4. Further references will be noted parenthetically.

2. Flood's claim that the reserve clause was unconstitutional because it amounted to the enslavement of the players by the owners, quickly made its way through the justice system, and in 1972 was rejected by the Supreme Court by a 5 to 3 vote. Nevertheless, the process Flood set in motion led to a challenge of the reserve clause a year later by the Players Association; and in 1976 the talented pitcher Andy Messersmith won his court challenge, leading to the institution of free agency for all professional baseball players and the acknowledgment of their legal right to consultation on any trades within certain clearly defined limits related to their playing time. Though his challenge ultimately transformed professional baseball, and despite his acknowledged talent, Curt Flood was never again given a chance to play in the major leagues.

3. Roth has made significant revisions in *The Breast*. We cite the 1980 revised edition, published in *A Philip Roth Reader* (New York: Farrar, Straus, 1980), 483. The passage is also found in the Penguin paperback edition (1985) 88.

4. Roth, *The Great American Novel* (New York: Holt, Rinehart, 1973) 87. Further references will be noted parenthetically.

CHAPTER SIX

Virtuoso Performances:
My Life as a Man (1974); *The Professor of Desire* (1975)

My Life as a Man

In *My Life as a Man* the narrator, Peter Tarnopol, and his fictional persona, Nathan Zuckerman, have fulfilled the obligations expected of them by their families. But being a good Jewish son has not prepared either of them for finding emotional, sexual, creative, or intellectual happiness in adulthood. Like Alexander Portnoy, Peter and Nathan are successful in their work: Portnoy is the Assistant Commissioner for Human Opportunity in New York City; Peter Tarnopol and Nathan Zuckerman, like Roth himself, have written award-winning novels while still in their twenties. Yet in their emotional and sexual lives they all believe themselves to be, and indeed are, failures.

In Roth's eighth work of fiction the narrator/author struggles self-reflexively to come to grips with the recalcitrant materials of his life. The novel is divided into two parts: "Useful Fictions," which includes two stories, "Salad Days" and "Courting Disaster"; and a long

VIRTUOSO PERFORMANCES

"autobiographical narrative," "My True Story," meant to be taken as Peter Tarnopol's account of his own life story. The title of the first part contrasts with the title of part 2; together they raise questions about the purpose of writing and the ability of fiction and/or autobiography to tell the truth. The novel itself begins with a note to the reader, stating that both parts are "drawn from the writings of Peter Tarnopol." The play of narrators moves from Tarnopol describing Zuckerman's early upbringing in the short "Salad Days," to Zuckerman's longer first-person narration in "Courting Disaster" of his disastrous marriage, then back to Tarnopol's own autobiography in "My True Story," which takes up more than half the novel. Throughout Roth dramatizes the narrator's shifting stance. The differences in the fictional and autobiographical accounts come to rest in the different intentions of these narrators and the differing purposes of the narratives.

Like Portnoy, Tarnopol feels compelled to tell his story or, more precisely, shape it into texts for interpretation as a means, retrospectively at least, of coming to terms with what he sees as a failure of manhood. He has allowed a disastrous marriage to reduce him to making the desperate gesture of donning his wife's undergarments to express his sense of emasculation at her hands. But neither through psychoanalysis nor through his recuperative attempts at writing "Useful Fictions" can he finally blot out that self-destructive image of himself. He cannot acknowledge his own complicity in the destructive dynamics of his marriage nor the hostility toward women, bordering on misogyny, that has fueled that collusion. For Peter Tarnopol, as for Alexander Portnoy, there are two basic questions: "How did I, a 'nice Jewish boy' with a youth so full of promise, make such a mess of my life?" and "What can I do to get out of this nightmare of frustration and impotence?" In *My Life as a Man*, Tarnopol seems to shift the blame for his predicament away from the claustrophobic Jewishness of his childhood, which Alexander Portnoy found so unmanning, to the combined highmindedness of the 1950s and a literary education in the classics of Western civilization. But in moving from Freudian psychoanalysis to pop sociology, Tarnopol is still looking for someone or something to blame other than himself. The coyly complex structure of the novel reveals that if Tarnopol has "been undone," it is because he has all by himself been "courting disaster," the title he gives Zuckerman's fictional account.

Tarnopol's Jewish upbringing informs both his "useful fictions" and his "true story." Virtually everything the protagonists in *My Life as a Man* do can be read as reactions to that crucial element of their childhood. In "Salad Days," the most lighthearted of the novel's stories, Tarnopol's fictive persona, Nathan Zuckerman, chooses Bass College because its image is so patently unlike that of growing up Jewish in Camden, New Jersey:

VIRTUOSO PERFORMANCES

It was the pictures in the Bass catalogue of the apple-cheeked boys in white bucks crossing the sunlit New England quadrangle in the company of the apple-cheeked girls in white bucks that had in part drawn Zuckerman to Bass in the first place. To him . . . beautiful Bass seemed to partake of everything with which the word "collegiate" is so richly resonant.[1]

Bass, in other words, is an emblem not simply of collegiality but of acceptance into the heretofore alien world of Gentile America.

As a student in Miss Caroline Benson's English honors seminar, Nathan is taken to task for his "relentless use" of the word *human:* "human character, human possibility, human error, human anguish, human tragedy. Suffering and failure . . . were 'human conditions,'" which Miss Benson finds "redundant" and "mannered," but which Nathan finds absolutely necessary (17). For him the word *human* replaces the insistent litany of his childhood: Jewish character, Jewish anguish, Jewish tragedy. Under Miss Benson's tutelage Nathan decides to drop out of Bass College's only Jewish fraternity, and learns to pronounce the *g* in "length" and the *h* in "whale." He writes an undergraduate honors thesis on "Subdued Hysteria: A Study of the Undercurrent of Agony in Some Novels of Virginia Woolf" as a way of channeling his upbringing and temperament into an enterprise acceptable to Miss Benson and everything she stands for. She had hoped that upon graduation Nathan might continue his studies at Cambridge or Oxford, but after a summer of licentiousness with Sharon Shatsky, the seventeen-year-old-daughter of Al, the "Zipper King" Shatsky, Nathan is drafted into the army. Roth's satire focuses on how Tarnopol and his fictional persona cannot escape the conflict between their ethnic identity as Jews—the specific ways in which they exist as human beings—and their gender identity as men. Jewishness shapes their masculinity in ways that can lead either to "Salad Days" or, just as likely, as it turns out, to "Courting Disaster." The tale ends ominously, before, as the narrator puts it, Nathan, "looking for trouble, . . . would find it" (30).

In Tarnopol's next "useful fiction," significantly entitled "Courting Disaster," Nathan and Sharon have broken up, and he is teaching creative writing in night school in Chicago. Zuckerman explains that he is drawn to one of his students, the woman who ends up making his life hell, because her Gentile background is the very opposite of his own comparatively sheltered and loving Jewish upbringing, against which he is reacting: "Not only that she had survived, but *what* she had survived, gave her enormous moral stature, or glamor, in my eyes: on the one hand, the puritan austerity, the prudery, the blandness,the xenophobia of the women of her clan; on the other, the criminality of the men [her father has raped her]" (70). Nathan's sister Sonia has also developed a taste for non-Jews, but she prefers Italians with shady backgrounds, who are immigrants like their parents, rather than mainstream Americans. After her first husband kills himself (Nathan suspects that he had attempted suicide without thinking it would actually work), she marries another much like him, prompting Nathan to wonder "if perhaps she were involved in a secret and mysterious religious rite: if she had not deliberately set out to mortify herself" (39). As it turns out, in abandoning Jewishness for the moral challenge Lydia represents for him, Nathan gets less rather than more than he bargained for. As he himself later concludes, he has squandered his manhood on Lydia. He has chosen her out of his own perverse desire, not out of love or lust, but to fulfill, rather than defy, that favorite dictum of Jewish parents, "Never marry a *shikse*." Thus Nathan's (and Peter Tarnopol's) rebellion against his parents is defeated by the fact that he, like Portnoy, is more his parents' son than he cares to acknowledge.

Lydia ends up killing herself, and Nathan runs off to Italy with her sixteen-year-old-daughter, who had been living with them after they won a long, drawn-out custody battle with Lydia's first husband. Daughter and stepfather remain in exile, living together now as lovers. Nathan is haunted by the spent possibilities of his youth and, as he tells his perverse story, keeps trying to decide to leave his stepdaughter and his shame and return to America. He can only conclude that though like his sister he has not really chosen freely but has only defied his parents, his rebellion has backfired.

Despite its title "Useful Fictions" fails to root out

Nathan's or Tarnopol's despair. Much of the discussion of the problems of his writing is an effort by Tarnopol to avoid facing up to his difficulty in telling the truth about his own disastrous marriage. "My True Story," the last section of this novel, begins with Tarnopol established at the Quahsay Colony, a foundation-supported artists' retreat where he has written the two stories "Salad Days" and "Courting Disaster"; now, after six months' contemplation he has decided to compose an autobiographical narrative. This third section begins with an italicized biography of Tarnopol written in the third person by Tarnopol himself. In it he states that he has been a patient of Dr. Spielvogel, the same psychoanalyst who treated Alex Portnoy. Spielvogel, an expert on creativity and neurosis, sees Tarnopol as one of "the nation's top young narcissists in the arts" (100).

Tarnopol then attempts to tell the "True Story," of the "nice civilized Jewish boy" who gave up the nice civilized Jewish Dina Dornbusch because she was "rich, pretty, protected, smart, sexy, adoring, young, vibrant, clever, confident, ambitious— . . . [but] a girl still" (178). What he really wants, he's decided, is "a woman" who has lived and suffered and can therefore make him "humanish: manly, a man" (173). Like Portnoy, what Tarnopol here implies is that the experience of having grown up "a nice Jewish boy" is somehow not conducive to the development of a full masculinity. The only way for him to compensate for the deficiencies of his Jewish boyhood is like Zuckerman to take on a *shikse* in defiance of his parents. With this non-Jewish wife he can tap into American masculinity and become "a real man" by all-American standards. Tarnopol titles the first section of his story "Peppy," the nickname his family used for him. In it he shifts back and forth from the nervous breakdown he has at twenty-nine in his brother's apartment in New York City as a result of his disastrous marriage to Maureen, contrasting that with memories of earlier days in his family. Tarnopol, we learn, is the youngest of three children of first-generation Americans. His father is a shopkeeper, his mother a homemaker. Tarnopol's older brother, Moe, is a radical professor at Columbia and a pragmatist very different from both his sister, Joan, and "Peppy." Joan, the middle child, five years older than Peter, had been homely and quiet, a good student who was valedictorian of her high school class. She had been determined to succeed, transforming herself through plastic surgery and a college degree from the University of Pennsylvania into an attractive and powerful woman, and had married a handsome, very successful professional man. They spend money lavishly and, what for Tarnopol is even more astonishing, his sister has accomplished all this and is "on such good terms with pleasure" without guilt (108). She invites Peter to stay with her in California. Instead of visiting, he sends her the two stories, "Salad Days" and "Courting Disaster," and she returns them with her own comments as well as those of an editor friend and his wife.

In part 2 of "My True Story" Peter describes his postbreakdown, postmarital relationship with Susan Seabury McCall. Submissive, cool, elegant, wealthy, and upper class, she is for Tarnopol the very opposite of his ex-wife, Maureen. Nevertheless, by the time he writes his "True Story" at Quahsay, his three-year relationship with Susan has been over for a year. Her history of breakdowns has led him, in what he thinks is self-preservation, to refuse to marry her. Both are emotionally broken individuals: Peter by his debasing marriage to Maureen, Susan by her strict upbringing and her love for her now-dead father. At first Peter and Susan had healed each other. Peter has calmed down and, at his urging, Susan has gone back to finish college at thirty. But Moe sees the relationship as repeating Peter's mistakes with Maureen, and Tarnopol's refusal to marry Susan seemingly confirms his brother's diagnosis.

Attempting to approach the central and most disturbing part of his "true story," his marriage to Maureen, Tarnopol launches into a critique of the sexual politics of the 1950s. According to Tarnopol, masculinity in the '50s was defined as "Decency and Maturity, a young man's 'seriousness'" (169). What underlies it is "the myth of male inviolability . . . male dominance and potency"; whereas femininity is characterized by female dependence—"that sense of defenselessness and vulnerability" (172). The effect of these gender definitions, he realizes, is debilitating for both sexes. As a result of

this social construction of their supposed relations, neither men nor women can marry for positive reasons.
Women feel the necessity of marrying to gain financial
and emotional support; while men feel the obligation
to marry in order to provide women with "equality and
dignity" (169). Thus, according to Tarnopol, women
were set up by the idea of marriage in the 1950s as the
perennial helpless victims, and men, as a result of this
ideology, became their all-powerful victimizers. But
Tarnopol takes issue with this dynamic. His argument
echoes Roth's response to feminist critiques of his work;
and at the same time, Tarnopol suggests, as does the
philosopher Hegel in a famous comment on the relations of master and slave, that the master, or victimizer,
is enslaved to the victim and unable to break the chains
of his bondage.

In offering his readers a scathing critique of marriage in the '50s, Tarnopol momentarily steps out of the
persona of autobiographer. He attempts to account for
what happened to him in his marriage by extrapolating
from it to a widespread cultural phenomenon. But his
exposure of the marriage rites of the 1950s is ultimately
more self-serving than illuminating. Though he goes
on for another 150 pages trying to figure out how and
why he could have become so enslaved, he never ade-
quately explains it. Yet his readers recognize, as Tarnopol does not seem to want to, that he has ended up
exactly where he thought he wanted to be: in taking on
Maureen he indeed purges himself of any pretensions

to being "a nice civilized Jewish boy." When he cannot get the best of her in any other way, he beats Maureen, aping his real American male counterparts, her abusive father and the first of her two former husbands, thereby achieving an American standard of masculinity. Ironically, however, for Tarnopol as for Portnoy, breaking the taboo turns out to be as disastrous as honoring it had been. Tarnopol finds that physically abusing Maureen, rather than enhancing his masculinity, actually unmans him. Whereas Portnoy's pursuit of *shikses* would seem to be motivated by his love/hate relationship with his mother and his unvoiced fear that marrying a Jewish woman will do to him exactly what his mother has done to his father—that is, unman him— Peter Tarnopol chooses a Gentile woman seemingly because she will indeed ultimately emasculate him. His choice of a marriage partner thus completes a perverse self-fulfilling prophecy about women. Thus, though they would appear to be motivated by exactly opposite reasons, Tarnopol's attempt at reconciling his Jewishness and masculinity is really no different from Alexander Portnoy's, nor any more successful. For both men the net result is impotence and frustration rather than a successfully negotiated masculinity.

Roth has described his male protagonists as "clay with aspirations," and claimed that his intention in his novels has been "to show the frailty and vulnerability of men" rather than to "demonstrate causes for male chauvinism."[2] The difficulty with this claim, however, is that "the frailty and vulnerability of men" and the "causes for male chauvinism" are rarely mutually exclusive. Indeed it is precisely male "frailty" that often fuels male chauvinism, encouraging men to turn upon and oppress those even less powerful than themselves, particularly women. Though the inadequacies, neuroses, guilt, and obsessions of Roth's protagonists would seem to be offered in mitigation of their misogyny, the dynamic is more complex and more destructive of those caught up in it than Roth's remarks might suggest. While his protagonists are frail, sensitive, literary, and demasculated by comparison with the powerful, physically bullying conventional image of the American male, Peter Tarnopol and Nathan Zuckerman, like Alexander Portnoy, at times recover their masculinity by oppressing non-Jewish women. In oppressing the women who belong to those ideal American males, these Jewish men get back at the supposedly all-powerful American males through their powerless representatives.

Roth's protagonists are part of the twentieth-century literary tradition of nonheroes. They are neither enfranchised and thus able to function as citizens, nor physically gifted and thus able to function out of pure gender definition. By comparison with the conventional image of the American male, they are failed sexual acrobats and guilt-ridden neurotics. The conflict between their Jewishness and the dominant ideology of American machismo compounds the collapse of their traditionally modest form of masculinity. Yet as Roth works through the nexus of Jewishness and masculinity from *Portnoy's Complaint* through *My Life as a Man* to *The Professor of Desire*, he moves away from any easy projection of blame or guilt to a fuller comprehension of his protagonists' sexual politics and their complicity in their own emotional and sexual dilemmas.

The Professor of Desire

Early in *The Professor of Desire*, David Kepesh, while a student at Syracuse University, comes across a description of Addison's collaborator in *The Spectator*. Steele, Macaulay says, is "a rake among scholars, a scholar among rakes." To Kepesh this motto becomes a "prestigious justification for" his "high grades and base desires."[3] Like so many of Roth's protagonists Kepesh feels himself split between the demands of "the Jewboy" and "the nice Jewish boy": he lives in his head, yet his body clamors for attention. Often he feels it virtually impossible to reconcile the conflicting demands of temptation, appetite, and aggression on the one hand, and repression, respectability, and social acceptance on the other.

The characters who surround David in the novel are paired to play out that conflict. In his youth David must choose between his "nice" parents and the scatological Herbie Bratasky. When he is an adult, it is the

repressed, respectable Schonnbrunn who stands in opposition to the "rapacious" Baumgarten.[4] During his fellowship year abroad he is tempted by both the loving
but ordinary Elisabeth and the uninhibited Birgitta.
Later he must choose between Claire, who is nurturing,
and sensually abandoned Helen. Yet David Kepesh's
sense of the necessity of choosing only exacerbates the
conflict. He sees himself as someone who must make a
series of either/or choices, constructing his life out of
decisions between extremes. *The Professor of Desire*, like
Portnoy's Complaint and *My Life as a Man*, suggests that
there is something inadequate in the opposed directions
into which its male protagonist feels himself split. Kepesh, like Portnoy, Zuckerman, and Tarnopol before
him, ends up going to destructive extremes before coming up with even a potentially workable solution—
which, however, is more than any of his predecessors
have managed. Attracted to both extremes, unable to
choose between the permissible and the forbidden,
Kepesh defines himself as a professor of desire, a wish-
ful, rather than a satisfied, participant/observer.

In all three of these novels and progressively more
explicitly, so that it is clearest in *The Professor of Desire*,
the female figures the protagonists encounter challenge
male control and the conventional, opposed categories
into which the protagonists feel themselves split. Because these novels are all either first-person narratives
related by their male protagonists, or omniscient narratives allied to the point of view of the hero, the reader

never knows what the female characters think. Their subjectivity is not present, or at best is unrevealed. But for the male protagonists they both attract and threaten, the females seem to represent a challenge to their masculinity, calling into question male complacency, power, and control. Thus the female characters become, in this male-centered discourse, the projection of the protagonists' doubts about themselves, implicitly posing the questions those males force the females to represent: What is masculinity? What *do* men want? For David Kepesh—as for Alexander Portnoy, Nathan Zuckerman, and Peter Tarnopol—those questions are not readily answerable.

David Kepesh's childhood is immersed in the rich pageantry of Jewish life at the Hungarian Royale, his parents' small all-kosher hotel in the Catskills. At college he becomes an actor who specializes in the imitation of some of the more colorful characters connected to the Royale. Perhaps because he seems only to be doing what he learned from Herbie Bratasky, David becomes disillusioned with the artificial life of the theater. By the end of his college career David Kepesh has become a "sober, solitary, rather refined young man devoted to European literature and languages" (12).

Like Portnoy, David remembers his mother as the more powerful of his parents, her competence and conscientiousness legendary, his father's dependence on her a given of his childhood; unlike Portnoy, David remembers growing up happy and loving, and neither condemns nor vilifies his parents for their differences from accepted gender definitions or for their too great love of him. Yet like Portnoy, Zuckerman, and Tarnopol, the choices David makes, his intellectual interests, the girls he pursues, point implicitly to a turning away from the Jewishness of his background. But with David the resentment shown by the others is gone. He makes his decisions less in reaction to his parents, whom he loves without any sense of blame or disenchantment, or in rebellion against a smothered childhood and adolescence, than from his own needs and desires. Still, again like Portnoy, Zuckerman, and Tarnopol, though he turns away from the "nice Jewish boy" model of masculinity, with its underpinning of social acceptance, he finds the "American" alternative no more palatable. Like his only male companion in college, the homosexual Louis Jelinek (who is also Jewish), Kepesh avoids dormitory living because he considers its "rituals of [male] camaraderie . . . contemptible" (17). In this way he separates himself from the ideals of American masculinity as well as from the Jewish communal values of his youth. The remaining alternative is the "Jewboy's" pursuit of appetite; but it hasn't worked for Portnoy, and it doesn't work for Kepesh either.

After college Kepesh is awarded a Fulbright grant to study Arthurian legends and Icelandic sagas in England, a boon for the nice Jewish boy in him. He almost immediately overthrows all his good intentions, however, by involving himself in a *ménage à trois* with two

Swedish girls, Elisabeth and Birgitta. After a particularly perverse evening together Elisabeth can no longer take the emotional pressure of the triangle. She is involved in an accident and returns, both physically and emotionally broken, to Sweden. Kepesh continues his liaison with her friend Birgitta, all the while assuring Elisabeth of his love in carefully composed letters and fantasizing about eventually marrying and having children with her. Hitchhiking around Europe with Birgitta at the close of his fellowship year, David lets her know that he plans to return to America without her. Birgitta packs her knapsack and leaves him to his regrets:

And then gently, so very gently (for despite being a girl who moans when her hair is pulled and cries for more when her flesh is made to smart with a little pain, despite her Amazonian confidence in the darkest dives and the nerves of iron that she can display in the chancey hitchhiking world, aside from the stunning sense of inalienable right with which she does whatever she likes, that total immunity from remorse or self-doubt that mesmerizes me as much as anything, she is also courteous, respectful, and friendly, the perfectly brought-up child of a Stockholm physician and his wife), she closes the door after her so as not to awaken the family from whom we have rented our room (45–46).

Kepesh pays her the kind of tribute he would perhaps like to have paid to himself. For him she is someone

who has reconciled her sexual predilections and her upbringing, the Swedish, female, equivalent of the Jewboy
and the nice Jewish boy. Thus she is powerful and in
control, whereas he feels how difficult it is to choose
between them. In deciding to return to the States to
pursue an academic career without "temptation," he
underscores his failure to reconcile what he experiences
as basic, yet unassimilable, aspects of his character.

Not surprisingly, once back in America Kepesh
finds that graduate school alone is not enough to sus-
tain him. When he first meets Helen Baird, he is attracted to her in ways that echo his attraction to Birgitta:

I begin at last to relinquish some of my suspiciousness,
to lay off a little with my interrogations, and to see these
passionate performances as arising out of the very fear-
lessness that so draws me to her, out of that determined
abandon with which she will give herself to whatever
strongly beckons, and regardless of how likely it is to
bring in the end as much pain as pleasure. . . . It appears
then that the capacity for pain-filled renunciation joined
to the gift for sensual abandon is what makes her appeal
inescapable . . . this beautiful and dramatic young heroine, who has risked and won and lost so much already,
squarely facing up to appetite (61, 64).

As the "heroine" of "passionate performances" Helen
is at the center of her own drama. Like Birgitta, though
unlike David, she is capable of giving herself over

wholly to whatever is at hand. But at least from David's perspective there is a difference between them: while Birgitta acts autonomously and participates in David's fantasies only incidentally (she has plenty of her own to occupy her both before and during their relationship), Helen is a "dramatic heroine" who, though she thinks she consults only her own tastes, in fact fulfills expected roles in relation to men rather than for herself. Despite hesitations on both sides they make a doomed marriage. Helen cannot let go of her fantasies while, in the face of the demands of everyday existence, David can no longer hold on to his. His masculinity is undercut by the "passionate performances" that had once so stimulated it.

After the collapse of their marriage Kepesh is temporarily on his own in New York. He develops a friendship with a faculty colleague, Ralph Baumgarten, as a way of filling part of his need for companionship. Baumgarten, who, though he happens like David to be Jewish, is, like Birgitta and Helen before him, "someone on the friendliest of terms with the sources of his excitement, and confidently opposed to—in fact, rather amused by—all that stands in opposition" (135). Though in David's eyes Baumgarten's family history is full of the kind of vivid pathos that could be transmuted into poetry and win acclaim for Ralph, he refuses to milk his past for the sake of success. Instead he prefers sexual adventures for their own, not poetry's, sake. Kepesh suspects his own motives in associating with

VIRTUOSO PERFORMANCES

Baumgarten, and realizes that he is playing out the appetitive Jewboy side of himself vicariously through him. One night after dinner at their favorite Hungarian restaurant, he and Ralph pick up a high school girl at a bookstore and take her back to Ralph's apartment to pose for them. Together they coax and coach her into various positions and stages of undress. Their interaction, as David reports to his psychiatrist, Klinger, two weeks later, is consensual. When she stops them and will go no further, the game is over. What Kepesh never confesses to Klinger is that their *ménage à trois,* which binds him to Baumgarten and asserts male power and prerogative, also makes him a secret sharer with Klinger himself, whose daughter—a photograph on Klinger's desk lets Kepesh know—was the very girl he and Baumgarten were with.

David is as ambivalent about Baumgarten as he has been about Birgitta and Helen. Though he is attracted by their capacity for giving themselves over to sensuality without guilt, for him the Jewboy/nice Jewish boy dichotomy can no longer be resolved simply by favoring one side of the equation to the exclusion of the other. The encounter with Klinger's daughter echoes Kepesh's longer triadic association with Birgitta and Elisabeth. It also leads him back to his loving childhood. Unable to sleep one evening in response to his father's whispered warning that his mother is dying of cancer, he imagines himself getting into bed between them, just as he had as a little boy. For David this position, caught up in so much love, is supreme.

In his imagination he achieves a pleasure denied his heroes, shameless Ralph, Helen, and Herbie. Their appetitive eagerness and aggressive exploration of desire are ideals Kepesh longs for as much as his parents' affection and love. While his muddling efforts to play both roles and be both nice Jewish boy and Jewboy yield mocking laughter, the joke turns out to be at the expense of Helen, Ralph, and Herbie, who despite their passionate performances never can quite fulfill their desires. Herbie Bratasky does not succeed outside the Catskills; Helen is only a stage star in the minor theater of David's classroom and apartment; and Ralph can't bring his seductions to consummation. Like Portnoy, Ralph and Herbie live inside Jewish jokes, which they tell to prove their manhood but, in fact, reveal them to be loud-mouthed *schlemiehls.* By contrast David Kepesh is not an aspiring Groucho Marx but the hero of a Woody Allen film, discovering through the tutelage of these passionate actors how to be a wiser, smarter, but still nice Jewish boy.

In Claire Ovington, Kepesh meets the first woman to whom he has been attracted since the end of his marriage. Unlike the sensual and exotic Birgitta and Helen, Claire is very much an all-American girl, complete with parents who appear to be just like those on the radio shows Alex Portnoy so enjoys, but whose alcoholism and constant fighting, more like the destructive ma-

chismo of the "real American fathers" in *My Life as a
Man*, point to the underside of the American dream.
Several months into their relationship David describes
Claire to his analyst in terms very different from those
he had used to delineate the fascinations of Birgitta,
Helen, and Ralph: "She is to steadiness . . . what Helen
was to impetuosity. She is to common sense what Birgitta was to indiscretion. I have never seen such devotion to the ordinary business of daily life. . . . There's
no dreaming going on there—just steady dedicated *living*" (158). Kepesh refers to Claire as "his rescuer," and
finds that "her sane love" has not only helped to heal
him psychically, but returned him to intellectual pro-
ductivity as well. By the end of their first year together,
however, as they travel through Europe, memories of
Birgitta disturb his equilibrium, heralding the waning
of his passion for Claire. By the novel's conclusion Kepesh feels that it is only a matter of time before the man
that he has become with Claire "will give way to Herbie's pupil, Birgitta's accomplice, Helen's suitor, yes, to
Baumgarten's sidekick and defender, to the would-be
wayward son and all he hungers for" (252). But he understands, as Portnoy, Zuckerman, and Tarnopol have
not, that if he is to be "robbed of Claire" and his life
with her, he cannot look beyond himself for an explanation: "It always comes down to myself!" (261). And it is
this acceptance of his own complicity in the collapse of
his relationships—his understanding that it is his own
failure to reconcile the Jewboy and the nice Jewish boy,

his taste for the exotic and his longing for the American, that causes his griefs and woe—which sets him apart from Roth's earlier heroes.

Notes

1. Roth, *My Life as a Man* (New York: Holt, Rinehart, 1974) 12. Further references will be noted parenthetically.

2. Judith Paterson Jones and Guinevera A. Nance, *Philip Roth* (New York: Ungar, 1981) 7.

3. Roth, *The Professor of Desire* (New York: Farrar, Straus, 1977) 17. Further references will be noted parenthetically.

4. See Barbara Koenig Quart, "The Rapacity of One Nearly Buried Alive," *Massachusetts Review* 24 (1983): 590–608, for an elaboration of this characterization of Baumgarten.

CHAPTER SEVEN

Boundaries: *The Ghost Writer* (1979); *Zuckerman Unbound* (1981); *The Anatomy Lesson* (1983); "The Prague Orgy" (1985)

In the novels that make up the trilogy published as *Zuckerman Bound*, Roth brings forward questions about the power of art that had previously served as background. Now sexual initiation and a young man's education are subsumed within the exploration of the writer's role and vocation. As Nathan Zuckerman searches for his identity as an artist, he discovers the meanings of familial and communal obligations. Not only are these central to his writing, he comes to realize that they are in fact the building blocks of his personality, which are inscribed upon his body. "You must change your life"—the quotation from Rilke which concludes *The Breast*—serves here as transition: it is the informing motif of the trilogy.

UNDERSTANDING PHILIP ROTH

The Ghost Writer

Roth begins with the twenty-three-year-old protagonist, Nathan Zuckerman, who is "writing and publishing my first short stories," embarking upon a visit to the "maestro" of literature, E. I. Lonoff. Nervous Nathan, apprehensive at the prospect of the eagerly awaited meeting, approaches the house of the great man by self-consciously imagining himself to be the hero of a *Bildungsroman*. Conflict and disappointment with his father have brought Zuckerman to see Lonoff. Nathan hopes to resolve his personal and artistic crisis by becoming Lonoff's spiritual son, petitioning for his moral sponsorship and hoping to gain "the magical protection of his advocacy and his love."[1]

Nathan wants to give both literature and life their due, but discovers that they make conflicting and irreconcilable demands upon him. Still, Zuckerman, the young artist, believes that literature can redeem life. He therefore decides to make a pilgrimage to the source of American art. At its altar and American center in the New England woods he hopes to find the truth and rededicate himself to the higher moral purposes of art. However, he knows that literary and biological fathers are not commensurable. Neither can replace the other; both place demands and responsibilities upon the son.

This quandary is central to all the novels in which he figures, including the *Zuckerman Bound* trilogy.

BOUNDARIES

Of course, I had a loving father of my own, whom I could ask the world of any day of the week, but my father was a foot doctor and not an artist, and lately we had been having serious trouble in the family because of a new story of mine. He was so bewildered by what I had written that he had gone running to *his* moral mentor, a certain Judge Leopold Wapter, to get the judge to get his son to see the light. As a result, after two decades of a more or less unbroken amiable conversation, we had not been speaking for nearly five weeks now, and I was off and away seeking patriarchal validation elsewhere (9–10).

Rejected by his immediate family, Nathan turns for a time in this novel to the symbolic world of art for personal validation.

Lonoff's stories have made such an impression on Zuckerman that he is eager to meet their writer, just as Lonoff has found Zuckerman's stories so intriguing that he has invited Nathan to visit him. Both writers seek to explore the connections between art and life, and to find out if personal acquaintance will yield greater insights into their art.

Zuckerman thinks of Lonoff, writing about the isolation of the modern Jew in his stories so arduously pursued through so many drafts, as an artistic role model. Severe to a fault, Lonoff's spare style and minimalist subject matter nevertheless help him reach the central concerns of American Jews like Nathan's parents. Nathan characterizes Lonoff's style as a "celebrated blend of sympathy and pitilessness." It grants authority "to all that is prohibitive in life" yet responds to "the same burden of exclusion and confinement that still weighed upon the lives of those who had raised me, and that had informed our relentless household obsession with the status of the Jews" (14, 12). Thus, Nathan reveres him both as an artist and as a potential spiritual father.

Reflecting on the achievement of the master, Nathan encounters the possibilities of the disciple. He notes that Lonoff's mastery of the grim facts of modern Jewish history is a source of pride to him as a potential spiritual son:

The pride inspired in my parents by the establishment in 1948 of a homeland in Palestine that would gather in the unmurdered remnant of European Jewry was, in fact, not so unlike what welled up in me when I first came upon Lonoff's thwarted, secretive, imprisoned souls, and realized that out of everything humbling from which my own striving, troubled father had labored to elevate us all, a literature of such dour wit and poignancy could be shamelessly conceived (12).

Lonoff's English prose, which often sounds to Nathan like a direct translation from the Yiddish, assimilates the vision of the insulted and injured, the humiliated, and the murdered. It brings new inspiration, pride, and power to American Jews. His work moves beyond concerns narrowly defined as Jewish to speak to the non-Jew about the conditions of modern life. "The typical hero of a Lonoff story," Zuckerman notes,

the hero who came to mean so much to bookish Americans in the mid-fifties, the hero who, some ten years after Hitler, seemed to say something new and wrenching to Gentiles about Jews and to Jews about themselves, and to readers and writers of that recuperative decade generally about the ambiguities of prudence and the anxieties of disorder, about life-hunger, life-bargains, and life-terror in their most elementary manifestations—Lonoff's hero is more often than not a nobody from nowhere, away from a home where he is not missed, yet to which he must return without delay (13–14).

Wrestling with these moral difficulties, Lonoff's unassuming hero cannot take decisive action—or else, acting boldly for once, he miscalculates and makes everything worse.

In characterizing Lonoff's work, Nathan seeks to define his own. Though they share similar themes and concerns, Nathan discovers that while Lonoff prunes away at style and subject matter like a latter-day Henry James, he himself is more Dickensian. Lonoff values control, while Nathan trades in exuberance. Like a ventriloquist Zuckerman prefers to present his characters self-consciously in their own tonalities. Despite their stylistic differences Zuckerman must wrestle with the possibility that Lonoff's fictional world accurately and completely describes his own life. His first-person narration in *The Ghost Writer* registers the events of the novel, seamlessly moving from a discussion of the writer himself to a complex consideration of his art.

As a city boy visiting the country in search of enlightenment, Nathan begins to wonder what there is for him to learn in this rural setting seemingly isolated from the burdens of modern history. But that is exactly the point: the social and political context of modern life makes its weight felt by its very exclusion. Lonoff has retreated from the urban Jewish world to the snowy fastness of the Berkshires and the New England world of American literary fastidiousness because he believes it is a haven from the totalitarian Nazi terror of twentieth-century history. "My guess was," thinks Nathan,

that it would take even the fiercest Hun the better part of a winter to cross the glacial waterfalls and windblasted woods of those mountain wilds before he was able to reach the open edge of Lonoff's hayfields, rush the rear storm door of the house, crash through into the study, and, with spiked bludgeon wheeling high in the air above the little Olivetti, cry out in a roaring voice to the writer tapping out his twenty-seventh draft, "You must change your life!" (27).

BOUNDARIES

The comic intrusion of the menacing medieval Hun is ironic Zuckerman's comment on the differences he perceives between Lonoff and himself.

Nevertheless, Zuckerman wants to create a mythology that, like Lonoff's, will honor the lives of his parents and their immigrant American generation, as well as his own brash and exuberant experiences as a native Jewish son. Having published a series of stories that have won him literary fame, along with rejection by leaders of the Jewish community, Zuckerman hopes to find in Lonoff's work and life a way of responding to the accusation that his stories are anti-Semitic. Unlike Lonoff, however, Nathan feels he cannot retreat in the face of the cruel history of the twentieth century. Lonoff's literary project, Nathan implies, despite its allegorical sweep, is narrow and confined. By contrast, Zuckerman's enterprise is a voyage into both the heart of darkness and the light of civilization: it is simultaneously heroic and hilarious. What Zuckerman must encounter in this odyssey of laughter and sorrow is the darkness in the light by which this wintry scene is illuminated.

The journey that began as Zuckerman's effort to find a literary father to replace the father of his Jewish origin launches him instead into the effort to bridge the two very different worlds he lives in—Newark and New England, Jewish urban history and American literary vocation, contemporary Jewish writers and American literature. To his surprise Zuckerman realizes that both poles are present in Lonoff himself. Born Emanuel Isadore Lonoff, he has become a Jewish Henry James, married to Hope, the daughter of an old New England family, in whose ancestral mansion they live.

In the course of their conversation Lonoff toasts Nathan, calling him "a wonderful new writer." Zuckerman imagines this literary judgment will rescue him from his family crisis. They discuss several possible literary forebears for Zuckerman, including the handsome, dashing, suave Abravanel—a fictional character who is a mixture of Saul Bellow and Norman Mailer, and Lonoff himself, whose literary portrait draws on elements of Bernard Malamud and the Yiddish American writers, the Singer brothers, Israel Joshua and Isaac Bashevis. Each of these figures, Zuckerman points out, is linked by a "family resemblance" to Isaac Babel: they are all the Russian writer's American cousins. Abravanel writes about "big-time Jews," an extension of Babel's fascination with "Benya Krik and the Odessa mob: the gloating, the gangsters, all those gigantic types" (47, 48). At the other end of the spectrum Lonoff's world focuses in an ironic mode on the *schlemiehl*—the little Jew—rendering his situation as victim in a powerful visual and lyric extension of Babel's response to his own crisis-ridden era in the Russia of the early twentieth century. "'And what about you?'" Lonoff surprises Zuckerman by asking. "'Aren't you a New World cousin in the Babel clan too?'" Though Zuckerman tries to evade the question, he voices his true response to himself:

But Lonoff had read my designing mind, all right; for when I came upon Babel's description of the Jewish writer as a man with autumn in his heart and spectacles on his nose, I had been inspired to add, "and blood in his penis," and had then recorded the words like a challenge—a flaming Dedalian formula to ignite *my* soul's smithy (49).

Zuckerman challenges himself to create an encompassing art: his writing will have to be explicitly American, Jewish, and male. In Nathan's work the Jew will be both *schlemiehl* and powerful Benya Krik, both pariah and parvenu. Thus Zuckerman's work will bring together the major roles of the twentieth-century Jew.[2]

Nathan comes to realize that no matter how ambivalent, even anti-Semitic his portrayal of Jews may seem, Jewishness is still the literary and moral center of his work. All of Nathan's literary mentors are Jews who take their Jewishness very seriously. The justification of art for its own sake that Henry James and Lonoff represent in the story will not suffice. Zuckerman cannot turn his back on the world; he needs both his actual and his spiritual fathers to realize his identity.

In the second chapter of the novel Zuckerman rethinks the claim he has made for Henry James and the moral stature of high art. Against that he weighs the understanding of what his father calls "ordinary people" and the demands of his community. Faced with this fundamental moral dilemma, Zuckerman realizes he has sought guidance from Lonoff because he has written about people trapped in the nets of history and thereby provided an extraordinary understanding for their ordinary lives.

The chapter title, "Nathan Dedalus," reminds the reader that Roth's novel of education echoes James Joyce's *Portrait of the Artist as a Young Man*. Furthermore, the references to Daedalus, who in Greek mythology sought to escape an island prison by fashioning wings and taking flight, provide an additional level of allusion. Like Stephen Dedalus in Joyce's novel, Nathan Zuckerman, a.k.a. Nathan Dedalus, may seek to fly too high and run the risk, like the mythological Daedalus' reckless son Icarus, of getting his wings melted and falling into the sea.

Writing about his Newark Jewish community, Nathan has been accused by its leaders of the worst kind of anti-Semitism. To them he is not only Icarus but the wicked son of the Passover Haggadah, who removes himself from the community.[3] Their condemnation has confused Nathan, calling into question his self-justification as an artist for whom art is the whole truth of life. Like Nathan's father, Judge Wapter, a Zuckerman family friend and pillar of the Jewish community, believes that in the public world he is an American, but in the privacy of his own home and community he is a

BOUNDARIES

Jew. Nathan's writing about the gritty side of lower-class Jewish life challenges their compartmentalization of the public and private by refusing to segregate American from Jewish realms.

Imagining he would soar on the wings of literature to the greatest heights, he finds himself instead poised to fall. As Nathan's father puts the case to him:

It's not your fault that you don't know what Gentiles think when they read something like this. But I can tell you. They don't think about how it's a great work of art. They don't know about art. Maybe I don't know about art myself. Maybe none of our family does, not the way that you do. But that's my point. People don't read art—they read about *people.* And they judge them as such. And how do you think they will judge the people in your story, what conclusions do you think they will reach? Have you thought about that? (92).

Neither Judge Wapter nor Nathan's father are entirely wrong in believing that most people make no distinction between fiction and autobiography. Novels and real stories, fiction and fact are often judged by the same standards. Yet for Nathan to accept the implicit demand that he censor his artistic vision for the sake of protecting the public image of Jews would paralyze him as a writer.

After weeks of silence Nathan's desperate mother calls to ask why he hasn't answered either the judge's letter or his father. Nathan responds by pointing out

Wapter's gross error. To treat art instrumentally and lump him with Streicher and Goebbels is to make Nathan Zuckerman into one of the most demonic anti-Semites of twentieth-century history. Nathan, the clear-thinking American, cannot sit still in the face of the judge's and his parents' confusion. "'We are not the wretched of Belsen! We were not the victims of that crime!'" Zuckerman protests (106).

What Nathan encounters here is the paranoia of twentieth-century Jewry, which, he is willing to acknowledge, has its basis in recent Jewish history. Nathan emphasizes the differences between America and Eastern Europe, present and past, in order to disentangle himself from the folkfear and the limited vision on which it feeds, just as Stephen Dedalus had to unravel the nets that tied him to the narrowness and mediocrity of Irish middle-class life. Nathan, however, must also answer the charge that he is a slanderer of the Jewish community and nothing but an anti-Semitic Jew. Is he only a modern version of the *malshin*—the informer?[4] Dramatizing the problems facing the American Jewish writer as he confronts the political and instrumental definition of art, Roth makes Zuckerman explore the meanings of his own role as a Jewish, American, and male writer. At the same time Roth indirectly pokes fun at those naïve readers who insist upon identifying the artist with his fictional creations, as many of his own readers did in assuming *he* was Alexander Portnoy.

Confronted by the irreconcilable difficulties of

BOUNDARIES

American art and Jewish life, Nathan spends a sleepless night in Lonoff's study, drafting letter after letter to his father. When masturbation does not relieve his anxiety, he turns to reading the Henry James story "The Middle Years," which centers on an aging writer's affirmation of the passion and madness of art. Suddenly he hears voices above him. He climbs on top of the desk, using the volume of James to attain the necessary height to eavesdrop on the master. Amy Bellette, Lonoff's protégée, has been visiting; now she tries to seduce him into running away with her to Florence. Lonoff soothes her, calling her the great survivor, and treating her as his daughter, a role she agrees to yet sexualizes. "I wouldn't be your little girl over there. I would when we played, but otherwise I'd be your wife" (119). To Nathan's astonishment Lonoff refuses to leave his wife, and he and Amy separate. This reality makes Nathan's imagination suddenly seem thin to him: "Dad-da, Florence, the great Durante, her babyishness and desire, his mad, heroic restraint—Oh, if only I could have imagined the scene I'd overheard! If only I could invent as presumptuously as real life!" (121). At this point, Zuckerman turns to his maleness for a way of resolving his problems. His male power—"the blood in his penis"—will get him out of this Jewish and American confusion.

The need for legitimation that has brought him to visit Lonoff, sparked by what he has overheard, leads Zuckerman to proceed to create a life history for Amy—

the attractive, exotic, former student of Lonoff's, who has a head too large for her body and a hint of a foreign accent. Zuckerman's fiction-engine moves into high gear, and he decides Amy is in actuality Anne Frank. Amy Bellette/Anne Frank did not die in the death camp but survived its torments. Overcoming the obscene human misery of Belsen and Auschwitz, which deformed her body so that her head remains larger than her frame, she is, in Zuckerman's eyes, a living example of the modern encounter with "Ultima Thule."[5] Having been recalled to life she discovers, Zuckerman imagines, that her diary has been published and has made her famous to the point where she is unable to resume her past life. And Lonoff, Nathan believes, shares Amy's secret: *That* Anne Frank is dead; *this* Amy Bellette, Lonoff's protégée and a brilliant writer who can "capture the place in a sentence," yet lives (28).

Zuckerman imagines that Amy will rescue him by accepting his offer of marriage, thereby irrefutably proving his Jewishness to his parents, friends, and relatives. "Throughout breakfast, my father, my mother, judge and Mrs. Wapter were never out of my thoughts," he muses at the beginning of chapter 4, near the end of his stay with the Lonoffs.

I'd gone the whole night without sleep, and now I couldn't think straight about them or myself, or about Amy, as she was called. I kept seeing myself coming back to New Jersey and saying to my family, "I met a marvelous young woman while I was up in New England. I love her and she loves me. We are going to be married."

The statement sets up the punch line. " 'Married? But so fast? Nathan, is she Jewish?' 'Yes, she is.' 'But who is she?' 'Anne Frank' " (157–58). Nathan goes on to visualize the scene in which he introduces Amy to his family, whereupon his father will be forced to admit his mistake in thinking his son a wicked slanderer of his people. *"Well, this is she" I said. " 'Anne,' says my father— the Anne? Oh, how I have misunderstood my son. How mistaken we have been!' "* (159). Rescuing him from the accusation of literary anti-Semitism, this fantasized marriage, Nathan imagines, will also reconcile him with his father. For Nathan to marry Anne Frank is to propose that he must deal with the Holocaust in his work and life as the defining event of modern times. It becomes the ever-present force demanding, through Rilke's poem, that he change his life.

The presence of Amy/Anne as Nathan's muse validates his exuberant American writing as a Jewish act. At the same time, their imagined marriage is a haunting metaphor for the relationship of the American Jewish writer and his people's European past. Thus Nathan accepts the fact that he will now become the ghost writer through whom his people gain their voice—the literary equivalent of their Jewish state, reborn Israel. The ghost of the novel's title here is doubled, referring both to Nathan as ghost writer and to the ghosts of all those murdered Jews who will speak through him. His American/Jewish art will redeem the European past.

Through this male initiative Nathan will be empowered by his community, serving as its representative. In speaking for it, his writing will fulfill traditional Jewish views of the obligations of its male members—though by conventional American standards writing is not a masculine art. What Zuckerman does not yet see is that Amy's misproportioned body and head link her as well to the ruined archaic torso of Apollo in Rilke's poem, whose powerful presence insists in a wordless message to the viewer that he must change his life. In this comic world, however, Nathan's imagined marriage with Amy/Anne is preempted by the eruption of a family quarrel.

In the final chapter, "Married to Tolstoy," Hope accuses Lonoff of being a monument of literary patience, who has seen her hair grow white in his service, without acknowledgment or gratitude. The necessary solitude of Lonoff's version of the literary life surprises Nathan, as does its potential cannibalization of all the writer's connections and relationships. Nathan takes the opportunity of Hope's rushing upstairs to insinuate to Amy that he knows she is Anne Frank. But she flatly repudiates the suggestion.

BOUNDARIES

But, alas, I could not lift her out of her sacred book and make her a character in this life. Instead, I was confronted by Amy Bellette (whoever *she* might be), turning the pages of Lonoff's magazine, and, while she savored his every underlining, waiting to see if at the last minute he would not change his life, and hers with it. The rest was so much fiction (171).

As the novel comes to a tumultuous climax, Amy/Anne and Hope all rush out of the house in the middle of a blizzard with Lonoff in pursuit.

In response to the offer of help from Zuckerman, Lonoff tells him instead to start writing about what he has witnessed. "There's paper on my desk. . . . I'll be curious to see how we all come out someday. It could be an interesting story. You're not so nice and polite in your fiction. . . . You're a different person" (179–80). Separating the writer from the tale, Lonoff's comment returns to the problems with which the novel began and the conviction that in life as well as art, now inextricably intertwined, there are no simple solutions, only more interesting questions.

As an artist Nathan has the responsibility of telling the truth about his community in his fiction; as a son he must face the consequences of that truth-telling. In *The Ghost Writer* Nathan Zuckerman completes the trajectory begun by Alex Portnoy. Zuckerman's narration and his encounter with Lonoff parallel Portnoy's going to Dr. Spielvogel for psychoanalysis and relief from his obsessive monologic recounting of his achievements and errors. Sons confessing to surrogate fathers, both seek the blessing that will allow them to honor their American desires while becoming once more welcome members of their Jewish community.

Zuckerman Unbound

Nathan Zuckerman's predicament in *The Ghost Writer* continues in *Zuckerman Unbound*, *The Anatomy Lesson*, and "The Prague Orgy." *The Ghost Writer* was narrated retrospectively by Nathan twenty years after the incidents and emotions, encounters and fantasies, he describes occurred. In *Zuckerman Unbound* attention shifts to the narrative present of a middle-aged, successful Zuckerman, who owes his notoriety to a wild and wildly successful novel, *Carnovsky*, which, the text suggests, resembles nothing so much as Roth's own *Portnoy's Complaint*. The title page of *Zuckerman Unbound* includes a quotation from a letter written by *The Ghost Writer's* E. I. Lonoff to his wife about the difficulties of fame: " 'Let Nathan see what it is to be lifted from obscurity. Let him not come hammering at our door to tell us that he wasn't warned.' " *Zuckerman Unbound* also deals with other themes first raised in *The Ghost Writer*, carrying forward the exploration of what it means emotionally and geographically to have broken the bonds between father and son, husband and wife, the links between artist and man, his adult life and his roots.

The unpleasant side of success confronts Nathan in the first line of *Zuckerman Unbound:* " 'What the hell are you doing on a bus, with your dough?' " he is asked by a short young man in a new business suit. From that moment on, Nathan loses the possibility, which he had sought in the vastness of New York City, of remaining anonymous. The young man announces to the other riders that Nathan, "the guy who wrote *Carnovsky*" and has just made "a million bucks" is on the bus. Nathan, who has just moved to an apartment on the fashionable East Side, is going downtown to seek financial advice about what to do with all his money. Suddenly his luck and financial success have become as "baffling as a misfortune." Instead of freedom from worries about money, he discovers he must worry about having his "money make money." Instead of being able to "come and go as he liked, when he liked, without having to remember beforehand who he was," Zuckerman discovers that he is a celebrity (184–85).

Nathan gets off the bus, fearful that in the violent atmosphere of the "spring of 1969," when not only is Vietnam a "slaughterhouse" but "off the battlefield as well as on, many Americans had gone berserk" (187), those who dislike *Carnovsky* will attack him. No one actually does him physical harm, but people do accost him with their views of the novel. A smiling middle-aged woman comes up to him in a coffee shop to tell him that reading the novel has liberated her; the "long-haired guard" in the bank at Rockefeller Plaza asks if he can touch Nathan's coat. However, not all of Zuckerman's readers provide positive reinforcement. While he is walking through the park, a young mother "out with her baby and her dog stepped into his path and said, 'You need love, and you need it all the time. I feel sorry for you'" (189). In the Public Library "an elderly gentleman tapped him on the shoulder and in heavily accented English . . . told him how sorry he felt for his parents" (189).

Like many of Roth's earlier novels about the situation of the Jewish-American son/writer, *Zuckerman Unbound* raises questions about egoism and responsibility, the status of art and the artist, the relation of the artist to his work and to his Jewish, as well as his American, community. But in this novel the father who opposes the son is at first geographically removed to Florida and then dies, supposedly freeing the son from his apparent obligations to family and community. The heavy hand of his father no longer weighing upon him, Nathan expects he will be able to write without having to consider how it will affect those close to him, or the larger community implicated in and avidly following his career. However, the introduction to Alvin Pepler, a failed quiz kid from out of the collective past who serves as a "double" or shadow figure pursuing Nathan throughout the novel, calls into question any easy solutions the increasingly paranoid Nathan may have found to resolve the dilemmas which haunt him.

At a sandwich counter in Nathan's upper Manhattan neighborhood Pepler accosts Nathan. Then in a typical passive-aggressive exchange he thanks Nathan for putting Newark, their shared city of origin, on the map, proudly listing the accomplishments of the famous sons and daughters of Newark: "There's Mary Mapes Dodge" and "there is LeRoi Jones," but most of all "in literature we have got you and Stephen Crane, in acting we have got Rod Steiger and Vivian Blaine, in playwriting we have got Dore Schary, in singing we have got Sarah Vaughan" (193). Pepler chants their praises, sure that their accomplishments define Newark as an important cultural center.

Nathan is amused by Pepler, even when Alvin tells him he too is a writer and asks Nathan if he can recommend an editor. When Pepler finally identifies himself as "the Jewish Marine" (197), Zuckerman recalls Alvin's fame as a quiz show contestant. Alvin is still consumed by his loss to Hewlett Lincoln, a more glamorous contestant, which was planned, he claims, for anti-Semitic reasons. Eventually Hewlett was unmasked as a fraud who had been slipped the answers by the show's producers, but by that point the damage to Alvin had been done. Now Alvin seeks to set the record straight by writing a book about his experiences, even imagining it as a hit Broadway musical, which will vindicate his honor both as a Marine and as a Jew. He is convinced

it is this combination, undoing conventional stereotypes, that has led to his downfall. He is proud that he
has all the qualities expected of a Jew, being smart and
quick-thinking, yet he is at the same time a tough,
much-decorated Marine veteran of two wars.

Nathan finds it impossible to shake the dogged Pepler, who catches up to him in the street and engages
him in conversation about Frank Sinatra, another very
successful New Jersey boy. Alvin begins to boast about
his connections to Broadway, and even announces
without any hint of irony in his voice or words that a
musical will be made of the Six-Day War—the producers are thinking of asking Nathan to write the libretto.
Alvin also tells Zuckerman that he has learned from
what happened on the television quiz show that by contrast with "schlock," which is purely commercial, art is
"controlled, art is *managed,* art is always *rigged"* (218).
Alvin insists on buying Zuckerman an ice cream cone
like "a father on an outing with his darling baby boy"
(221). When he enters the store to buy the treat, Zuckerman seizes his opportunity and runs away. The focus
on food as a reward throughout this episode highlights
Alvin's unconscious emphasis on the ethnic connection
between Nathan and himself; the ice cream cone echoes
the New Jersey schoolboy links between these literary
doubles.

Nathan's encounter with Alvin threatens his
privacy, and he retreats to his apartment, his unlisted
telephone number, and his answering service. The un-

BOUNDARIES

wanted attention he has received makes Nathan wary. Now that he is famous, his personal life has become everyone's business; even Rochelle, who runs his telephone answering service, offers him unsolicited advice on investments. Without any prior notion of what success would entail, the wildly successful Zuckerman is disoriented by the unexpected reality: ordinary, everyday life has become overwhelming. Nathan realizes with a shock that he has not even unpacked the eightyone boxes of books he's moved into his apartment, though the walls of his new study have been furnished with custom-built bookshelves. Even the mail is more than he can deal with; every day there are nine or ten letters attacking him as an enemy of the Jews. Suddenly a voice on the phone, which he has picked up inadvertently instead of letting the answering service screen the call, demands "some of the money" (240). The caller knows his mother's address in Florida. "If you don't want her to disappear, you'll listen to what I have to say." In the middle of the harangue Zuckerman hangs up. Though reassured by Rochelle that the caller is probably just "some pervert" (241–42), he is shaken by it.

In thinking about the excesses his success seems to have forced upon him, Zuckerman is led to recall an earlier visit to Miami to prepare his mother for the deluge of reporters he knew, given the success of *Carnovsky*, she would have to confront. They had done some role-playing, and he had impersonated a reporter asking her about Nathan's toilet training to get her ready for the onslaught of questions. They had visited his father in the nursing home where he had been since his second stroke. His father had difficulty speaking and at times did not even recognize his wife. His visits have troubled his father, Nathan realizes, though he is perplexed about the cause. The other members of the family have been dragged into taking a stand for or against *Carnovsky* and into commenting on Nathan's upbringing—something his father has been spared. And Cousin Essie, Nathan remembers with pleasure, defended him when *Carnovsky* had been discussed at the Jewish Center.

At a Manhattan party Nathan meets and receives the approval of Professor Ellmann, the noted critic, and is introduced to the movie star Caesara O'Shea, "keeper of the screen's softest, most inviting lilt" (256)—who is an Irish movie version of Nathan. He writes about racy and raunchy immigrants; her box-office magic is the result of "all the sorrow of her race and then those splendid tits" (256). Zuckerman's gift for mimicking other people has not made it easier for him to find his own voice. This woman who can play many roles makes him see his own life differently. At thirty she fears what age will do to her. As Nathan consoles her, he begins to muse on his own youthfulness. She is reading Kierkegaard's *The Crisis in the Life of an Actress*, and he leafs through it while she is on the telephone. Comparing their respective crises, they begin to fall in love.

BOUNDARIES

The third chapter begins with Nathan observing the funeral of a gangland figure who has died, not in a spray of bullets, but from a cerebral hemorrhage. Then his mind reverts to the threats against his mother. It is Alvin Pepler, it turns out, who is behind the threats. Zuckerman's flight from Alvin and his refusal to write his life story for him has turned the ex-Marine against him. Now Pepler blames Zuckerman for all his failures. He reads *Carnovsky* as the boyhood he had always deserved but never had. In fact, Alvin claims, Nathan has gotten rich and famous by stealing the idea of *Carnovsky* from him. Instead of Weequahic, Zuckerman's school, the South Side high school Alvin attended taught him the realities of Newark. "Moron," Pepler screams at him in a personal confrontation. "To you" Newark is "Sunday chop suey downtown at the Chink's!" But the real city "is a nigger with a knife! Newark is a whore with the syph! Newark is junkies shitting in your hallway and everything burned to the ground!" Pepler is no longer the civic booster. He has exchanged the high-minded prose of his earlier list for the gritty language of the neighborhood in which he grew up.

Newark is dago vigilantes hunting jigs with tire irons! Newark is bankruptcy! Newark is ashes! Newark is rubble and filth! Own a car in Newark and then you'll find out what Newark's all about! Then you can write *ten* books about Newark! They slit your throat for your ra-

dial tires! They cut off both balls for a Bulova watch!
And your dick for the fun of it, if it's white (336).

The chapter title, "Oswald, Ruby, et al.," signals the
murderous violence Zuckerman feels emanating from
Pepler's rage. Nathan discovers that the anger of the
ex-Marine, like that of a friend who "taught English in
the New York school system for over thirty years,"
keeps people from seeing the difference between the
"illusionist and the illusion." Maybe, as he had said to
her, "you're confusing the dictating ventriloquist with
the demonic dummy" (348). The political violence of
their era has made it impossible for them to hold on to
everyday reality; it has become dreamlike. In the world
in which President Kennedy was assassinated, and his
assassin was then gunned down, everyone's fantasies
have been unbound.

The nightmare continues: In an envelope Nathan
finds the handkerchief he had given Pepler to dry his
hands with after Pepler had finished eating Zuckerman's sandwich. "There was no note. Only, by way of
a message, a stale acrid odor he had no difficulty identifying" (356). Masturbation, the activity Carnovsky practices obsessively in the novel, Pepler now engages in to
show that life imitates art. Then the phone rings but,
instead of announcing his mother's kidnapping, this
phone call tells Nathan his father has had a coronary.
He rushes to the hospital, where a family reunion is in
progress. Bending over the dying man, he catches his

BOUNDARIES

father's last word, "Bastard," but does not know to whom it refers.

Later, his brother Henry insists it is Nathan their father has cursed. The writer of *Carnovsky* is the bastard who has brought their father two strokes and an early grave. When Nathan protests that he had always been glad that his father had not been able to read *Carnovsky*, Henry tells him that the elder Zuckerman had known about the novel and had it read aloud to him. And *Carnovsky*, with its unbridled sexual energy and display, killed him, Henry insists. Then Henry too accuses Nathan of being a bastard—unrestrained and irresponsible, willing to do anything for his art, unwilling to acknowledge the simplest human obligations. "Everything is exposable! Jewish morality, Jewish endurance, Jewish wisdom, Jewish families—everything is grist for your fun-machine" (397).

The novel concludes with a stunned Nathan arriving at Newark airport. There he asks a taxi driver to take him to his old neighborhood. The apartment house he grew up in is now surrounded by a chain-link fence and inhabited by people to whom he is a nobody. In this place, now,

you are no longer any man's son, you are no longer some good woman's husband, you are no longer your brother's brother, and you don't come from anywhere anymore, either. They skipped the grade school and the playground and the hot-dog joint and headed back to

New York, passing on the way out to the Parkway the synagogue where he'd taken Hebrew lessons after school until he was thirteen. It was now an African Methodist Episcopal Church (404–05).

At last, and amid these ironic circumstances, Nathan has become unbound.

Nathan's education has progressed through the stages signaled by the titles of the novels that make up the trilogy *Zuckerman Bound*. In *The Ghost Writer* his identity as a man and a writer has come into question in his encounter with Lonoff and Amy Bellette, and he becomes the teller of someone else's tale. In *Zuckerman Unbound* financial success releases Nathan from the constraints of routine only to plunge him into personal confusions and the father's curse that threaten to destroy him. Now, in *The Anatomy Lesson*, he will discover how these experiences have left their traces on his body.

The Anatomy Lesson

This, the third novel in the trilogy, ironically brings this writer with "blood in his penis" to the discovery of personal limitations. Its five chapters—"The Collar," "Gone," "The Ward," "Burning," and "The Corpus"— successively strip away Nathan's defenses. As writer, lover, Jew, son, and friend he suffers from excess; he has too much of everything, beginning with success, and it all crumbles in the face of a mysterious pain in his shoulder, neck, and back. The roles he has so arduously constructed for himself cannot defend him against the primal pain that overwhelms him.

"When he is sick, every man wants his mother; if she's not around, other women must do. Zuckerman was making do with four other women," *The Anatomy Lesson* begins. "He'd never had so many women at one time, or so many doctors, or drunk so much vodka, or done so little work, or known despair of such wild proportions." Yet Zuckerman does not give in. Desperately he seeks strategies to relieve him of his excesses and his pain.

As he narrates the tale, Zuckerman finds he can describe what is happening to him but discovers it is almost impossible to step outside of the particular moment and locate the bits and pieces in a larger whole. Different doctors prescribe different cures. He demands of himself that he continue writing, only to discover it is an excruciating act. Various women he meets offer to help him; all make love to him. Jenny reads to him and bakes bread; Gloria complains about her husband's lack of sexual drive, buys groceries for Nathan, and fixes gourmet meals; Jaga works for the doctor who is trying to help him keep his hair and tells him about her unhappy life in the Bronx and her confused relationships in Warsaw; Diana, a young finishing school student, acts as his secretary and takes dictation while telling him of her abused childhood and her reluctant boy-

friend. In "intercourse, fellatio, and cunnilingus" with
them, and in taking pain-killing drugs, smoking mari-
juana, and drinking vodka Nathan discovers momentary relief (417). What he cannot find is the reason for
what is happening to him. One of the psychoanalysts
he visits suggests he is suffering because he is "the aton-
ing penitent, the guilty pariah," the "remorseful son,"
and "author of *Carnovsky*." Zuckerman is indignant:
"Expiation through suffering? . . . The pain being my
judgment on myself and that book?" and terminates the
therapy (430).

Sick Zuckerman relives his dying father's pain,
while longing for his mother. Since he wears an ortho-
pedic collar "to keep the cervical vertebrae aligned," he
opens his college English anthology to Herbert's poem
"The Collar," and reads its conclusion in which the son
accepts the father's law. Angered, he throws the book
across the room. "He refused to make of his collar, or
of the affliction it was designed to assuage, a metaphor
for anything grandiose" (412).

In the second chapter he recalls his mother's death
and his anguish. Going through her effects with his
brother's wife, Carol, he keeps a clipping his mother
had cut out; it describes Nathan as one of the famous
offspring of Newark. Nathan also treasures the piece of
paper on which, shortly after her final admission to the
hospital, she had written, instead of her name "Selma,"
"Holocaust."

When a note maligning his mother's memory is

BOUNDARIES

thrust into the mailbox, Zuckerman is enraged. His anger leads him to think about Milton Appel, a famous literary critic who first praised his work, then after *Carnovsky* reconsidered and damned him for vilifying the Jews. But now, just after the Yom Kippur War of 1973, Nathan learns through a friend that Appel wants him to write an op-ed piece for *The New York Times* in support of Israel. He recalls the attack Appel launched on him for saying "the Jews can stick their historical suffering up their ass" (491). Zuckerman looks up the quote from *Carnovsky*, only to find that it is the comment a fourteen-year-old boy, enraged at his family's obsession with their Jewishness, makes to his sister. Zuckerman is furious that a "licensed" literary critic, Appel, cannot distinguish between character and author, and makes the writer a scapegoat for his own fears. Despite the pain in his neck, arm, shoulder, and back, Zuckerman writes a four-page response to Appel.

In the third chapter Zuckerman's obsession with Appel's unjust attack upon him continues. He has, however, found temporary relief from his back pain by using a pillow invented by Dr. Kotler to relieve sufferers of exactly his condition. Kotler too is from Newark, and he tells Nathan of his love for the city and how the great Newark fire and riot of 1969 which destroyed it was for him as cataclysmic as the Second World War and the Iron Curtain. Now eighty, he has retired to New York; he reads the Bible regularly and visits the Metropolitan Museum to study Rembrandt's paintings. Inspired by

Kotler, who has a sense of the organic connections between body and mind and thus has become a "dolorologist"—that is, a doctor who tries to cure human sorrow and pain—Nathan decides to become a doctor and applies for admission to the University of Chicago medical school.

Nathan's decision to put aside his writing for a time and become a doctor is the result of a newfound sense of humility in the face of his chronic, difficult condition. He rejects the advice of his "comforters" that his pain is only the result of stress and tension and that he should learn to relax, repudiating the notion that his pain is self-inflicted because he is always finding "new ways to be unhappy" (439). The "crippling of his upper torso" is not, as they would have it, "the punishment called forth by his crime: mutilation as primitive justice" (440). There must be a different reason at work.

Nathan learns that Appel has telephoned. His anger returns and he calls the critic, spilling out his rage while defending his writing and his vision of modern life. He calls Appel "President of the Rabbinical Society for the Suppression of Laughter in the Interest of Loftier Values," branding him with the lofty, high-cultural values he espouses. This "Minister of the Official Style for Jewish Books Other than the Manual for Circumcision" enforces the fearful cultural establishment's perspective, like a literary Rabbi Binder (Ozzie Freedman's antagonist in "The Conversion of the Jews"), demanding that Jewish writers not exercise their rights as American citizens. Zuckerman insists that his books are serious. Unlike Appel's models, however, Nathan's work is rooted in the folk tradition of Yiddish culture which takes the encounters of everyday life in all its grittiness as its subject. Through the fictional title of *Carnovsky*, Roth connects his work with Israel Joshua Singer, who wrote an important novel with the same title.[6] Roth thereby aligns himself with the Jewish folk tradition against the high road of moralizing and ideologically oriented literary criticism.

Exploring the connections between intellectual and sexual life in *Carnovsky*, Zuckerman has revealed the origins of Jewish intensity, something Appel feels is a secret of the tribe. It is this, Zuckerman believes, that has infuriated Appel, who wants to keep Jewish writers in line. "Regulation number one: Do not mention your cock. You dumb prick!" Nathan exclaims (573). Attacking Appel, Nathan justifies his own life and work, and repudiates the claims of another literary "comforter." Though Nathan's anger exhausts him, it does provide him with some relief from his constant pain.

On the plane to Chicago to do his premed courses Nathan muses that feminists have treated him no better than the Jews. "They had put him on the cover of one of their magazines: WHY DOES THIS MAN HATE WOMEN?" (577). The man next to him in the airplane asks him what he does, and a distracted Nathan replies that his line is pornography: he publishes a magazine called *Lickety Split*. Taken with the idea, Nathan expands on it, and compares his magazine to *Playboy* and himself to Hugh Hefner. Asked his name, Nathan decides on revenge and says he is "Milton Appel. A-p-p-e-l. Accent on the second syllable. Je m'appelle Appel" (579). Nathan then recalls his undergraduate days at the University, and realizes that Chicago had liberated him from the constrictions of Jewish New Jersey but that fiction had "boomeranged him right back" (586). Perhaps his new career as a doctor will finally free him. In the meantime he will masquerade in Chicago as Appel, the liberator of the id. Nathan's desire for revenge consumes him. As the chapter ends, he realizes "he couldn't have stopped if he'd wanted to" (631). Zuckerman is out of control.

The serious side of the satire derives from the supposed unmasking of the somber arbiter of culture. By making Milton Appel a pornographer, Roth, the satirist, reminds us that for most male writers at least, pen and penis are linked.[7] *Carnovsky* was called pornography by Appel; now Zuckerman turns the tables on him: even the critic puts his pants on one leg at a time. Roth's satire is a way of hitting back at a cultural establishment that, like *Commentary*, first proudly published "Eli, the Fanatic" and then turned on him: when his explorations of Jewish communal life violated the sense of decorum of its editors, they excommunicated him. Roth is aware that in calling him an anti-Semitic and self-hating Jew, such critics fall into the net he has set for them in his work, which dramatizes the situation and psychology of the self-hating Jew.[8] What Roth understands, as Appel does not, is that in responding to the contradictions and varied possibilities of modern life, the self-hating Jew acts out what others have evaded. The method of ridicule in *The Anatomy Lesson* deflates Appel's pretensions by revealing what he has repressed in order to function as the liberal Jewish censor and arbiter of culture.

Roth's satire, however, is double-edged: Appel is not the only one who has been consumed by his professional pride. The price of Zuckerman's obsession with what others think of him is an enormous backache. This ache comes to represent his writer's block, a block and a pain so profound he can do nothing but lie on the floor and drink vodka to dull it, worrying all along that rather than having suffered too much, he hasn't yet suffered enough. As Roth himself notes,

Comedy is what Zuckerman is bound by—what's laughable in *Zuckerman Bound* is his insatiable desire to be a serious man taken seriously . . . Coming to terms with the profane realities of what he had assumed to be one of the world's leading sacred professions is for him a terrific ordeal—his superseriousness is what the comedy's about.[9]

Roth's satire does not let Zuckerman off the hook. The dangerous radical novelist gets writer's block. He who was always ready with a quick retort and a literary send-up is tongue-tied. *The Anatomy Lesson* comes to a conclusion as Nathan displaces his grief and confusion at the death of his mother onto Mr. Freytag, a friend's father whose wife has recently died. In the cemetery he assaults Freytag in a frenzy of disgust at his maudlin sentimentality. Nathan slips in the snow and breaks his jaw on one of the tombstones—ironic commentary engendered by the plot of the novel on this out-of-control talker.

His surgeon takes the opportunity of Zuckerman's broken jaw to wean him from his addiction to painkillers. Rendered helpless, unable to talk at last, Zuckerman is forced to meditate on what he has tried to do to himself. His thoughts return to Kafka, and he muses that Kafka's father was

the last of the old-fashioned fathers. And we . . . the last of the old-fashioned sons. Who that follows after us will understand how midway through the twentieth century, in this huge, lax, disjointed democracy, a father—and not even a father of learning or eminence or demonstrable power—could still assume the stature of a father in a Kafka story? No, the good old days are just about over, when half the time, without even knowing it, a father could sentence a son to punishment for his crimes, and the love and hatred of authority could be such a painful, tangled mess (686).

Nathan the son finds himself searching for the authority of the father, only to discover that primal power no longer exists. Instead of the law and punishment Nathan has found absurdity, comedy, and liberation. The result is the removal of boundaries and the mess of love and hate. Despite what others have told him, Nathan knows that his pain is not punishment for crimes against the father.

Nathan's meditations lead him to discover the meaning of the pain most human beings encounter. He faces his new vision, hoping as well to avoid it, "as though he still believed that he could unchain himself from a future as a man apart and escape the corpus that was his" (697). Here corpus refers both to the body of his written work and to his own body as the site of meaning. The satire of the novel ultimately directs itself at Zuckerman: it is *only* when his jaw is broken, resulting in excruciating physical pain that parallels and expresses his spiritual condition of being unable to speak, that Zuckerman can begin to confront his obsessive habits. Only then does he face the ultimate limitations of his body and his writing. Perhaps then he can begin the process of changing his life.

The anatomy lesson that has taken Zuckerman from his high-minded ideals back to the body that is his real self is also, like Robert Burton's *Anatomy of Melancholy*, an analysis of his depression, thus echoing one of the classics of seventeenth-century English literature. The account of his pain, the analysis of his writer's life and what it has been about, is both physical and metaphysical. What it has led Nathan to is the reliving of a modern version of Job's tale. Nathan too has discovered that the advice of his comforters is wrong; and like Job, at the conclusion of this tale in which the protagonist confronts human suffering, Zuckerman encounters one of the fundamental truths of the human condition.

"The Prague Orgy"

"The Prague Orgy" serves as an epilogue to the trilogy *Zuckerman Bound*, standing in ironic relation to the three novels that precede it. In it, a considerably more mellow Zuckerman has come to terms with his fame and fortune, but must now meet the challenge of Prague, Kafka's and Milan Kundera's city. From his privileged position Zuckerman views the deprivation and depravity of those who live under a repressive political regime "where the literary culture is held hostage." The dreamlike sequences of "The Prague Orgy" bring into bold relief the sexual politics of life in what Roth, in introducing a series of fictions by writers from Eastern Europe for Penguin Books, has designated as "the other Europe"—the world of the victims of modern war and totalitarian politics.

The political and psychological contradictions of modern life that have obsessed Nathan throughout the trilogy reappear on a different scale. In "The Prague Orgy" Nathan Zuckerman, author of *Carnovsky*, discovers that desire has a political dimension. The story's episodes echo the voyeurism of *The Professor of Desire*, where writers come to Prague to talk of Kafka. What Kepesh only dreams of—a visit to a prostitute Kafka frequented and the chance to fondle her—actually happens here. In the world of "The Prague Orgy" sexuality is defined by measuring the sexual organs, which are handled as if they were meat in a butcher shop. Kepesh sexualizes his world, while Nathan's reality, full of seemingly sexual encounters, is not in fact sexual but political. In the totalitarian society of Prague, where explicit political life is forbidden, erotic acts, Zuckerman discovers, are in fact political expressions. Politics has been driven into the erotic zone.

One of the reasons writing is so carefully monitored in Prague is that words determine reality in this world. In "The Prague Orgy" sexual contact is mediated by language: talking is more exciting, more real, than sexual intercourse, since words are more forbidden, more taboo, and therefore more desired than sex. In this Kafkaesque world literature is more real than life. It is worth noting that "The Prague Orgy" has received the highest praise from Eastern European writers, leading to the decision by Josef Skvorecky, the brilliant Czech novelist living in exile in Canada, to choose it, of all contemporary American writing, to translate into Czech.

The plot of "The Prague Orgy" turns on Zuckerman's effort to recover some Yiddish stories. An exiled

Czech acquaintance asks him to bring these stories, written by his father, a Jew murdered by the Nazis, to America, where they can be published. His estranged wife, who still lives in Prague, either has them or can help locate them. When Zuckerman meets Olga, he discovers that he himself is now part of a sexual/political game. Olga has the best legs in Prague, he is told; he finds out for himself that she is a central figure in the seemingly swinging sexual encounters of Prague's artists and intellectuals. First she tries to seduce him; then she brings him to a party where she initiates a young boy; then in conversation with Nathan she curses her former husband, and claims the story that his father was killed by the Nazis is a pious fraud; finally she demands that Nathan marry her and take her to America. She asks him how an American woman—a heroine of one of his novels, for example—would go about seducing him. Olga's directness and explicit sexuality, Nathan comes to realize, serve to hide rather than reveal the truth.

In this world everyone is alienated and practices a form of self-censorship, playing with the meanings of words till they turn into their opposites. Even those Czechs who live in the United States despise themselves, perhaps only slightly less so than their countrymen who continue to live in Prague. The disorientation of all these characters is reinforced by the form of "The Prague Orgy," which is a series of entries from Zuckerman's notebooks from January 11, 1976, to February 5,

BOUNDARIES

1976. The notebook entries are fragmentary; abbreviations are frequently used; episodes break off and others begin in the middle of the action. Zuckerman, the narrator, is himself a central character in the action, bringing events to their climax through his unwitting questions. Without an authorial voice the reader is left to put the pieces together, just as Zuckerman has to. What both have to decide is to what extent these words and this writing can be trusted to tell the truth.

As he searches for the lost bits of his own Yiddish past, Zuckerman moves through a landscape reminiscent of a spy story. A literary critic who wants to interview Zuckerman turns out to be an agent of the secret police. There are double crosses, threats, and counterthreats. Sexual invitations turn out to be bait for the commitment of literary indiscretions, which have profound political consequences. Zuckerman realizes this is not the world in which his impersonation of Milton Appel's rhetoric of sexual liberation could provide a measure of personal revenge without inflicting irrevocable damage. That version of pornography, which claims to free sexuality from any other value, is absent. Though sexuality is everywhere, it stands in Prague for everything except itself. Politics, which in this city has been forbidden, has been transmuted into eroticism, which has become the "only arena for freedom and self-realization"[10]

Political ideology determines everything in this country. In a restaurant, Zuckerman learns how the authorities have "used Anne Frank as a whip" to drive the mistress of his Czech friend from the stage. Here, to perform the role of Anne Frank on stage is to be branded a Jew-lover—in a nation that owes much to the Jews but has been for some time officially anti-Zionist. Under these conditions Anne Frank is not a great modern writer who tells the truth about totalitarianism but a "curse and a stigma" (759).

Nathan realizes that here "there's nothing that can't be done to a book, no cause in which even the most innocent of all books cannot be enlisted." While this is a political dilemma of modern life everywhere, it is in Prague that the idea is most thoroughly put into operation: "this place is proof that a book isn't as mighty as the mind of its most benighted reader" (759). In the face of the power of ideology and the modern state, literature becomes a political instrument and words become slogans. In Soviet-occupied Czechoslovakia there is no distance between the self and the roles one plays, whether in the theater or real life. Taking everything literally, everyone who uses words with any serious purpose, with any wit, is at risk.

As he maneuvers through Prague in search of the missing Yiddish manuscripts, Zuckerman makes another discovery. For him Prague's urban landscape is the repository of the Eastern European Jewish past: "This is the city I imagined the Jews would buy when they had accumulated enough money for a homeland." It is not that Zuckerman didn't know "about Palestine and the hearty Jewish teenagers there reclaiming the desert and draining the swamps, but I also recalled, from our vague family chronicle," these "shadowy, cramped streets" (760). The evocative architecture out-faces the totalitarian power of the modern state, leading Nathan to reimagine Prague as the Jewish homeland. In effect what Zuckerman finds is not the Jewish future of Israeli culture but the Eastern European Jewish past, which includes the Holocaust.

In Prague, he realizes, the "national industry" is "the construction of narrative out of the exertions of survival" (761). Everyone here is a talker, but nothing they talk about is as it seems. As a result, the Czechs lead him to recall the complexities of Jewish linguistic usage honed by centuries of oppression. Roth notes that the stories he hears build to a climax that requires an "uproarious punch line." The explosion of laughter is what makes the evident suffering all around him bear-able. Seeing the absurdity of it all, storytellers defend themselves with humor; it is what keeps them sane amid the unrelieved grimness of life in this other Europe. Roth's description evokes the gallows humor of the Holocaust, the stories and jokes that bear witness to the tenacious effort to resist the destruction of the thousand-year-old civilization of the European Jews by the Nazis in the 1940s; it points as well to the more recent destruction of the vital culture of Eastern Europe by the Soviet Union. "That such things can happen—there's the moral of the stories—that such things happen to me, to him, to her, to you, to us. That is the national anthem of the Jewish homeland. . . . Story-telling is the form . . . resistance has taken against the coercion of the powers-that-be" (762). In this world sto-rytelling is the most profound of all the forms of art, because these are stories inscribed in the human body. Here, "one's story isn't a skin to be shed—it's inescap-able, one's body and blood. You go on pumping it out till you die, the story veined with the themes of your life, the ever-recurring story that's at once your inven-tion and the invention of you" (782).[11]

Zuckerman finds the manuscripts of the Yiddish stories—only to have then confiscated by the secret po-lice. As they threaten him, he begins to understand the ways in which this ruined Prague stands for the intimi-dating past that expresses the inner condition of his life. While driving Zuckerman to the airport, Novak, the minister of culture, lectures Nathan on

how my father has expressed his love of country all his life. In 1937 he praised Masaryk and the Republic. . . . When Hitler came in he praised Hitler. After the war he praised Beneš when he was elected prime minister. When Stalin threw Beneš out, he praised Stalin. . . . Even when Dubček came in, for a few minutes he praised Dubček. . . . "Son, if someone called Jan Hus nothing but a dirty Jew, I would agree." These are our people who represent the true Czech spirit—*these are*

BOUNDARIES

*our realists! . . . people who know how to submit decently to
their historical misfortune! (780).*

This acceptance of double-think is the orgy the system
forces its people to engage in. Ideology transforms
meaning into political expediency. Words hide reality.
To keep them from asserting their truth someone bearing the power of language must be made into a scapegoat. The writer and the Jew join in fulfilling this role
for the ideologues whose propaganda mills churn out
the message: The "dirty Jew and Zionist," the writer
and intellectual, are to blame for it all. Thereby they
evade and repress the meanings of the murderous recent history of Eastern Europe. Like the security agent
at the airport who calls him "Zuckerman the Zionist
agent" (784), Prague makes Nathan discover the fullness and limitation of his identity at the same moment.

The world of this city serves as the architectural
embodiment of Rilke's enigmatic phrase, central to the
entire *Zuckerman Bound* trilogy. Prague reminds Zuckerman that in the face of the terror of the twentieth century, we must all change our lives. The form of the
"complaint" Roth perfected in *Portnoy* has now taken
on a more complex and profound dimension. In the
later works the question of the relationship of men and
women has a more historical and social context than it
did in his earlier work; the "complaint" is no longer a
kvetch, or a whine, but a moving meditation on contem-

porary history. Prague, the city not only of Kafka but of Rilke, of Kundera, and Skvorecky as well as Theodore Herzl, the founder of modern Zionism, has become the urban embodiment of the memory of the tragic possibilities of modern Western history.

Notes

1. Roth, *Zuckerman Bound* (New York: Farrar, Straus, 1985) 9. Further references will be noted parenthetically.

2. See Hannah Arendt, *The Jew as Pariah: Jewish Identity and Politics in the Modern Age*, ed. Ron H. Feldman (New York: Grove Press, 1978), for the most important statement of this distinction and its implications.

3. "What does this service mean to you?" (Exodus 12:26) the wicked or rebellious son asks. "By using the expression 'to you,' it is evident that this service has no significance for *him*. He has thus excluded himself from his people and denied God; therefore, give him a caustic answer and say: 'It is because of what the Lord did for me when I came out of Egypt.' (Exodus 13:8) 'For me,' not for *him*, for had he been there in Egypt, he would not have deserved to be liberated." *The Passover Haggadah, Ha-Haggadah Shel Pesach*, ed. Morris Silverman, rev. ed. (Bridgeport, CT: Prayer Book Press, 1975) 13.

4. In Mishnaic times the rabbis added a paragraph about the *malshin* to the central meditation of Jewish prayer, the Amida: "*Vela-Malshinim al tehi tikva* . . . May the slanderers have no hope; may all wickedness perish instantly; may all thy enemies be soon cut down. Do thou speedily uproot and crush the arrogant; cast them down and humble them speedily in our days. Blessed art thou, O Lord, who breakest the enemies and humblest the arrogant." *Daily Prayer Book*,

BOUNDARIES

Ha-Siddur Ha-Shalem, trans. Philip Birnbaum (New York: Hebrew Publishing Company, 1949) 87. Also see the discussion by Joseph H. Hertz, *The Authorised Daily Prayer Book* (New York: Bloch, 1955) 143–44, and the entry "Informers," *Encyclopedia Judaica* (Jerusalem: Keter Press, 1972) 8: 1363–73.

5. "Ultima Thule," a name from ancient mythology for the most northerly area of Europe, became for nineteenth-century American writers like Melville and Poe a figurative phrase indicating the most distant goal or remote land, and was usually associated with the frozen north. That snowy imagined destination evokes Melville's whale and Poe's maelstrom, and then comes to refer to the moral emptiness of the Nazi murderers of the Jews.

6. Roth may also be referring to the Yiddish actor Morris Carnovsky, a major figure in the American Yiddish theater.

7. See Sandra Gilbert and Susan Gubar, *The Madwoman in the Attic* (New Haven: Yale University Press, 1979) ch. 1.

8. See Sandor L. Gilman, *Jewish Self-Hatred: Anti-Semitism and the Hidden Language of the Jews* (Baltimore: Johns Hopkins, 1986), esp. the last chapter.

9. Interview with Philip Roth by Asher Z. Milbauer and Donald G. Watson, *Reading Philip Roth* (New York: St. Martin's Press, 1988), excerpted in *The New York Times Book Review* 4 Jan. 1987: 24.

10. Milan Kundera, commenting on the movie version of his *The Unbearable Lightness of Being,* in an interview; *San Francisco Chronicle Datebook* 31 Jan. 1988: 18.

11. Maxine Hong Kingston makes a similar point in *The Woman Warrior* (New York: Knopf, 1976) by emphasizing how her family's oppression has been inscribed on Fa Mu Lan's back.

CHAPTER EIGHT

Counterlives:
The Counterlife (1987)

In *The Counterlife* Roth carries the formal experiments of his earlier work, especially *My Life as a Man* and *The Ghost Writer*, to a new level of achievement. *The Counterlife* has no single central plot or story, no clear beginning, middle, or end. Each of its five sections describes a series of overlapping events, which are told from different points of view. Each first-person narration is interrupted and countered by a connected yet opposed account. Yet what a counterlife is, whether opposition to the majority culture or alternative life style, is not easily sorted out. Even at the very end of the novel this question remains open and incompletely determined. The subject of the novel, expressed in its title, itself becomes a central interpretive issue. The narrative organization places the burden of decision upon the reader. Providing a range of possibilities, Roth asks the reader to judge. Thus the novel's form expresses its content and poses the question: What, precisely, has or might have happened in this novel?

The Counterlife begins in the middle of the action

with a meditation by Nathan Zuckerman on the heart condition of his brother, Henry. The drug Henry is taking to control his hypertension makes him impotent. Nathan describes Henry's effort to respond to his situation, rendering his brother's conflicting swirl of thoughts and feelings. These ten italicized pages come to an end as Henry phones his brother. The narrative then switches to Nathan's thoughts, as Henry's voice disappears and Nathan's voice comes forward to describe Henry's funeral. Realizing that these first pages of the novel cannot serve as the eulogy for Henry which his grieving widow has asked him to deliver, Nathan apologizes to her. In response, Carol, the understanding sister-in-law, tells Nathan that the quarrel between the brothers doesn't matter any more. Yet this novel is full of persistent quarrels and irreconcilable points of view. Even the most peaceful scenes turn out to conceal bitter arguments. Roth presents the differences without providing conclusive readings, narrative closure, or authorial resolutions.

Not only do the three main characters each narrate large sections of the novel, they also comment on the accounts of the others in an effort to correct and reinterpret them. They accuse each other of betraying the most intimate secrets and quarrel about the meaning of particular incidents, including whether or not they in fact happened. Faced with their own deaths as well as those of their loved ones, each seeks the final word. Minor characters interrupt, claiming the right to tell their own stories; not only do they dwell on their life histories they also expound upon their views of the modern Jewish situation. Each character tells his or her own story in his or her own idiom, with its characteristic diction and inflection. Just as there are many narratives here rather than one dominant account, so there are many linguistic groupings in this pluralist, heteroglossic universe of discourse.[1] The fullness of detail of each of the narratives make each highly persuasive, but their contradictory qualities turn the novel into a hall of mirrors. Both structure and content lead to questions about the purposes of writing and storytelling. The reader is constantly asked to decide which of the accounts is true just at the moment when each calls attention to itself as a story, a fiction.

The novel further teases its readers with blurred lines of relationship among the various characters and between those characters and the different narrators who include them in their accounts. Is Maria Henry's former mistress, or Nathan's current one? Is she Nathan's potential wife, for whom he is willing to undergo the rigors of open-heart surgery, or is she a character in a pastoral fantasy he's written? Has Henry found himself and reclaimed his masculinity as a committed Zionist in Israel, or did he die on the operating table? Or does he, neither dead nor in Israel but alive in New Jersey, have the power in the novel's penultimate section to censor what would seem to be the dead Nathan's manuscript of *The Counterlife*? As for Nathan, the dominant figure in the novel, it is not clear at its conclusion whether he is dead or alive; whether he is married to Maria or only the creator of the fantasy of her cool English grace and intelligence, as well as the embattled reporter analyzing England's pervasive, if covert anti-Semitism.

The Counterlife offers Roth's enduring protagonist, Nathan Zuckerman, a spectrum of unusual possibilities. They challenge the realistic view of fiction, outrageously violating its conventions, but are nevertheless within the bounds of Nathan's persistent preoccupations. In this novel Nathan is a freewheeling bachelor and devoted husband and father; he is a lapsed, self-hating Jew and fervent American Zionist; he is a lover and father-to-be awaiting the birth of his son; he is a writer, a shaper of sentences, and through them a manipulator of real as well as fictional lives. Nathan encompasses the range of contradictory experiences of the novel, which are played out in New York and suburban New Jersey, Tel Aviv, Jerusalem and the Negev, London and the English countryside. None of them is abandoned; all of them are necessary to configure the perennial imaginings and realities of Nathan Zuckerman and his family.

Yet despite the fact that he occupies centerstage, Nathan's fictional status sticks to him. Roth makes sure his history as a character in a self-conscious fiction—as the protagonist of Peter Tarnopol's "Useful Fictions" in *My Life as a Man*—is present in this novel where he sounds so much like a real person. Thus, the question of how much of his life is "real," how much only "fiction," is not easily disposed of. In Peter Tarnopol's account of Nathan's life Nathan's preoccupation with his masculinity takes the form of an anxiety about his seriousness as an intellectual, an artist, and, covertly, as a Jew. But in *The Counterlife* Peter Tarnopol has disappeared, and Nathan is the writer of record. Instead of Tarnopol's effort to sort out what it means to be an intellectual, an artist, and a Jew, in *The Counterlife* these become different aspects of an ongoing quarrel. Furthermore, the relationship between Jewishness and masculinity is now complicated by the vexed question of the place of Israel and of anti-Semitism in the lives of American Jews and the non-Jewish world. Tarnopol's "useful fictions" have been translated in *The Counterlife* into several versions of similar stories that intersect, coincide, contradict, or tend to override each other but do not cancel each other out. Instead they now compound and multiply each other.

Nathan's self-absorption leads him beyond himself and his work to an obsession with his own death, heralded by that scourge of midlife masculinity, impotence caused by medicine he must take for his overworked heart. Each situation functions as a proposition leading to its counterlife. Roth dramatizes both what it means to be a modern Jew and what it means to seek to escape from the obligations of modern Jewish history. The novel details the power of sexuality and the escape from the oedipal drama. Nathan embraces the power of the imagination to make counterlives and repudiates it in favor of the reality of the everyday. Since none is given pride of place over the others, they become suspended alternatives. Each is one reading in what Nathan insists is not only a fiction but as well the book of life.

The Counterlife is divided into five sections: the titles of parts 1, 2, and 4 are names of places, and the titles of parts 3 and 5 are more generalized "places" or "spaces"; each title articulates the state of mind induced by the particular counterlife it suggests. The sections juxtapose wildly different alternative scenarios; the collision of contradictions forces the reader into the process of choosing potential conclusions for the novel.

"Basel," the first section, is the story of the choice Henry, Nathan's brother, must make between a long but impotent life with his wife and children—without the pleasure of indulging himself in daily oral sex with his dental assistant, Wendy—or the surgery which may kill him but which, if successful, will cancel the need for the heart medicine that induces his impotence. This section also harks back to the controversies surrounding the death of Nathan and Henry's father. In *Zuckerman Bound*, Henry accused Nathan of killing their father by publishing *Carnovsky*. Henry claimed that *Carnovsky* gave his father enough *tsuris*—troubles—to kill him. Many characters from the earlier novel reappear, from Cousin Essie, "cunning, shrewd, self-aware, another sort of survivor entirely," to Henry's devoted and competent wife, Carol, and their children. Other familiar figures of Roth's fiction make an entrance, including Herbert Grossman, "the Zuckermans' only European refugee." Like Mr. Barbatnik, the friend of the father of David Kepesh in *The Professor of Desire*, Grossman has gone through the hell of the Nazi death camps. Unlike Mr. Barbatnik, Grossman is not glad simply to have survived, and so cannot accept everyday life like someone who has come back to life from the world of the dead. Then there is Shimmy Kirsch, "the Neanderthal" brother-in-law and "arguably the family's stupidest relative." He is "one of those rapacious sons of the old greenhorn families who will not shrink from anything even while, fortunately for society, enslaved by every last primitive taboo"[2]. In Nathan's mind his very presence raises many of the questions—how to be a Jew, how to be human, how to be a man—that have haunted him and various other protagonists of Roth's novels all along.

Though they are members of an extended family, the Shimmys form a remarkable contrast to the Zuckermans' professional dignity. The Shimmys have no family tradition of doubt and self-consciousness; rather, theirs is the habit of seizing opportunities. Despite their differences, however, all of them are suspicious of Nathan's work as a writer, and all of them have at times blamed Nathan for giving Jews a bad name. Henry's death, with which this section of the novel begins, and the family gathering it results in, force Nathan to confront familiar preoccupations: Where do one's loyalties lie? Is one's first duty to oneself and one's art, or to those whom one's life touches and affects? Where does moral discrimination get us? If not earthly reward, is there some other kind of payoff? Like *My Life as a Man* and the *Zuckerman Bound* trilogy before it, *The Counterlife* raises questions about the writer's art, the conflict between the writer's obligations to himself and to others, and about "fiction's betrayal of life and the novelist's treachery to those who surround him."[3]

For Henry, as for his father and other Jews in the community, what Nathan does in "exploiting and distorting family secrets"—and, by extension, Jewish secrets—for his livelihood (10) is morally reprehensible. Henry's private solution is to redeem those whose secrets Nathan reveals by imagining "a kind of counterbook" to what Nathan writes. But Henry, who turns out in part 4 to be an astute critic of the dead Nathan's work, cannot in "Basel," the first section, control Nathan from beyond the grave. At Henry's funeral Nathan thinks to himself "that words that were morally inappropriate for a funeral were just the sort of words that engaged him." They are the ones that would reveal Henry's closest and most guarded secrets. Nathan cannot simply feel for his dead brother. "He was now going to have a very hard time getting through the day without seeing everything that happened as *more*, a continuation not of life but of his work or work-to-be" (13). His creative imagination stops at nothing, and he cannot keep himself from transmuting even Henry's funeral into art.

Everything in "Basel" hinges on choice. Each choice in turn leads to a particular counterlife. Should one be "strong and selfish," or "good"? Should one risk everything or play it safe? How many chances do each of us get to make a change, not so much for better or worse as for something different, a change that will counteract, or perhaps counterbalance, that which has preceded it? Thus choice becomes not simply something which people make or do, but a matter of alternative interpretations. The characters in the novel must choose between different readings (and writings) of open-ended situations:

Either what [Carol had] told everyone from the altar was what she truly believed, either she was a good-hearted, courageous, blind, loyal mate whom Henry had fiendishly deceived to the last, or she was a more interesting woman than [Nathan had] ever thought, a subtle and persuasive writer of domestic fiction, who had cunningly reimagined a decent, ordinary, adulterous humanist as a heroic martyr to the connubial bed (48).

The Counterlife never stays with one alternative for very long without raising the possibility of its opposite. It is a world of either/or as well as of if/then. As a result, the question of whether or not there are real alternatives in these characters' lives or just nuanced differences of interpretation remains open.

Basel, the Swiss city, is not only the home of Henry's rejected mistress but also the site of the founding of modern Zionism. Here Theodore Herzl gathered the Jews of Europe and America in 1897 to chart a new set of national possibilities for the Jews. These were to be realized in the land of Israel and the founding of the modern state of Israel in 1948, the locus of the next section, "Judea." More explicitly than any of Roth's earlier work, "Judea" engages the intense political questions of what it means to be a contemporary American Jew. In it Roth suggests that perhaps the cure for private impotence in New Jersey is a public rebirth—or counterlife—of renewed masculine and Jewish strength and vigor in Israel. There "the powerless, the scattered, the impotent Jews of the Diaspora are restored to potency by nationhood."[4] The American characters in "Judea" try out the possible counterlives available in the Jewish state of Israel in the post-Holocaust world, which they measure against the history of Jewish persecution, the destruction of European Jewry by the Nazis, and the institutionalized tolerance of the contemporary assimilationist, pluralistic United States.

Like Roth himself Zuckerman returns to an Israel he has visited once before. In 1960 Roth participated in a public dialogue between Jewish-American and Israeli writers on the subject of "The Jew in Literature," to which he was invited because of the controversy generated by his award-winning first book, *Goodbye, Columbus*.[5] In *The Counterlife*, Nathan's career parallels Roth's, and his version of *Goodbye, Columbus* is entitled *Higher Education*. Nathan recalls in *The Counterlife* that while in Israel on his first visit as a young writer, he defended what he called the "Zionism" of secularized, assimilated American Jews to his new friends, Shuki Elchanan and his father. *The Counterlife* plays Nathan's earlier visit against his later one. Nathan recalls his response to the Elchanans' insistence that Israel is the only place for Jews to make their home: American Jews are also committed Jews. From Galician peasants they have transformed themselves into writers and dentists, Zuckerman claims, thinking of the careers he and Henry are carving out for themselves in New York and New Jersey. For them Zionism is not living in the land of Israel but the "taking upon oneself, rather than leaving to others, responsibility for one's survival as a Jew" (53). Though it revises the ideals of the movement for the national liberation of the Jewish people by championing the individual achievements of American Jews rather than the communal Zionism of Jews in Israel, this Zionism is just as valuable and as viable, the young Nathan argues, as the classical Israeli version. Yet despite his assertion of American Jewish possibilities, Nathan had a picture taken of himself with then Prime Minister Ben-Gurion for his father to use "as ammunition" against those who would accuse him of anti-Semitism and Jewish self-hatred. (The passage also echoes the scene in

COUNTERLIVES

The Ghost Writer in which Nathan imagines himself marrying Anne Frank to prove to his Jewish critics, especially his own father, that though he is an American he is also a committed Jew.) To all this the elder Mr. Elchanan, a welder from Haifa who is also a member of the Knesset, Israel's parliament, responds that while Israel is a Jewish theater, Nathan lives in a Jewish museum. The implication is clear: Nathan should leave his private American life and take up his historic Jewish responsibilities in Israel.

"Judea" continues as a more mature Nathan returns eighteen years later to ask for Shuki's help in finding his brother Henry, who has forsaken an impotent life in the Jewish museum of the New Jersey suburbs for a renewed and newly vigorous life in Israel, the Jewish national theater. Nathan has returned to Israel at his sister-in-law's request to reclaim his brother, newly converted to messianic Zionism, and bring him back to this wife and children in New Jersey. His old friend Shuki is as skeptical as ever, though now even more disillusioned. He asks Nathan—whom he refers to as "the Jersey boy with the dirty mouth who writes the books Jews love to hate" (64)—a question central to Nathan's, and not incidentally Roth's, work: "Why do you pretend to be so detached from your Jewish feelings? In the books all you seem to be worrying about is what on earth a Jew is, while in life you pretend that you're content to be the last link in the Jewish chain of being" (73). Nathan has no answer except to quip,

"Chalk it up to Diaspora abnormality." But Shuki has shifted ground in eighteen years, and now this answer will not do. For him it is Israel in the 1980s that has become the home of the abnormal, the "American-Jewish Australia." Full of social misfits and religious fanatics, it has become "the Jewish obsessional prison par excellence!" (77). Despite its condition, or perhaps because of its exuberant excess, Shuki, though a trenchant critic of his people, cannot turn his back on this homeland he both hates and loves. For the moment Shuki has become Nathan's Israeli alterego.

A more frontal mode of defending Israel, however, falls to Mordecai Lippman, the novel's most vocal advocate of Zionist and Jewish/Israeli manifest destiny. For Lippman and his followers, including a newly religious and Zionistic Henry Zuckerman, who call to mind the movement for the Greater Land of Israel, the State of Israel must exist because anti-Semitism is always just around the corner. Like contemporary prophets they foretell a time in the not-too-distant future when American Jews, victims of persecution by people of color in the United States who have been urged on by the white anti-Semitic ruling class, will flee to Israel by the millions. For the Israelis in the West Bank settlement in which Henry and Lippman live, half of whom are American-born and raised, embracing their identity as Jews is a political choice. To them the skepticism of a Shuki Elchanan or a Nathan Zuckerman can only be a form of Jewish self-hatred. To Lippman these areas are Israel's by biblical right; to Shuki and Nathan, who call them by their current Arabic geographical names, the West Bank and Gaza, they belong to those who have made their recent homes there.

Henry then tells Nathan, in yet another reflexive moment, that he is leaving behind the "narcissistic past" and the psychologized soul-searching of Nathan's heroes for

a larger world, a world of ideology, of politics, of history—a world of things larger than the kitchen table, . . . a world defined by *action*, by *power*, . . . a world outside the Oedipal swamp. . . . Here you fight, you struggle, here you worry about what's going on in *Damascus!* What matters isn't . . . *any* of that crap you write about— *it's who runs Judea!* (140).

Nathan, however, can't shake the idea that Henry's real motivation for embracing Zionism with such fervor is his recent sexual frustration, which led him to the dangerous heart surgery. Compensating for his earlier inability to leave the confining obligations of his suburban marriage to Carol for a counterlife with his Swiss-German mistress, Maria, Henry, Nathan believes, has chosen to make a radical break with his past and really change his life. Nathan suspects that Zionism in Judea is Henry's only "unchallengeable means to escape his hedged-in life," the only rationale with a moral force equal, even superior, to that of his obligations to his wife and family.

For Henry going to Israel provides a new vital and vigorous self. Recalled to life by the fictional strategy of the novel, Henry now lives in his ideal world. Judea is heaven for him, a place where for the first time in his life he can stake out his claim to his own land and his own self.[6] To Henry his Zionist counterlife is enabling and empowering, even if it is at the same time, as Nathan implies, a simplistic response. Yet Henry's new life is a distinct possibility in Israel, Nathan realizes, for this is a country where everything is written in capital letters. As Shuki puts it, "Here everything is black and white, everybody is shouting, and everybody is always right" (64). Nathan shows a grudging admiration for this place where the quarrels are all out in the open. Still, for him Israel—too Jewish, too absolute—lacks perspective. Will war and guns finally replace culture in besieged Israel, Nathan wonders? While he finds the atmosphere heady, he is certain there is no place in Israel for someone of his temperament. Nathan believes himself to be too skeptical, too irreverent, too individualistic, and too American to fit in.

For Nathan the strident political arguments of Israel are not enough. He has another side, which opens up the possibility of a different counterlife for him. Nathan, the American-Jewish intellectual and writer, values listening as much as speaking. But Shuki, Nathan's Israeli

alter ego, mocks him for being too patient. Shuki believes that Nathan listens so intently because he doesn't
really care for Israel and Jewish life. As Shuki says,
Nathan has the charm and *savoir faire* of a Frenchman,
and his secretly desired counterlife is not that of a Zionist in Judea but that of an English country squire living
the life of gentility with the Gentiles in England.

In "Aloft," the third section of the novel, Nathan
is in an airplane, leaving Israel and musing about his
failed mission to bring Henry back to New Jersey. He
takes the opportunity to read a letter from Shuki.
Nathan's problem, Shuki tells him in yet another of the
novel's reflexive passages, is that he is "a writer with a
strong proclivity for exploring serious, even grave, subjects through their comical possibilities." He has an in-
clination to be "funny and ironical about things one is
supposed to be *for* or *against*, . . . even the Jew's vulnerable situation" (157–58, 161–62). Shuki points to
Nathan's gift for comic hyperbole and notes that when
put into play in the face of overwhelming danger, it
produces a dangerous cynicism. There are situations in
which, Shuki implies, this kind of comedy is out of
place. Ironic Nathan, however, believes in the complexity of modern art; for him there are no easy solutions.
Nathan thinks of writing Shuki to express all that he's
left unsaid while in Israel. Then he re-reads a letter to
Henry which he has been unable to complete, in which
he articulates the parallel between Henry's counterlife
of potent manhood in Israel and the Diaspora Jew's pos-

sible counterlife of potent Jewishness in the United States, where Jews can be Americans as well as Jews. While Nathan acknowledges that for Henry as for Lippman life in Israel is indeed the Jews' only true counterlife, he also warns Henry that life is not so simple and straightforward. Israel, Nathan points out, was conceived of as a utopian place where Jews were to go so they could forget who they were. They would "un-Jew" themselves: there will be "no more Jewy Jews," Nathan says, making his communal name into a sarcastic epithet that distances himself from his own ethnic, religious, and national identity. Nathan insists that "the construction of a counterlife that is one's own anti-myth" is at the very core of the Zionist movement for the national liberation of the Jews (147). Now, feeling his argument against Henry's Zionism becoming self-justification that legitimates his own choice of the Diaspora counterlife, Nathan claims that even the original Zionists, wanting to purge themselves of the bitter Jewishness of exile, functioned like Jewish anti-Semites. They too were infected with the modern Jewish self-hating virus, which is invading his own thoughts and feelings. And yet Nathan is forced to acknowledge that his brother—whose "obverse existence" his own existence posits—is a version of Nathan himself. Henry's counterlife is Nathan's own anti-myth. To Nathan, nothing Henry does is totally alien—just as Israel with its extremes and Henry's choice of a fuller Jewish life there for a counterlife are a part of Nathan. These choices emerge as insistent, contradictory, and raucous voices engaged in ongoing arguments inside Nathan's head.

At this point the bespectacled rabbi sitting next to Nathan in the airplane engages him in conversation. The rabbi turns out to be a disguised Jimmy Lustig, a Jew from New Jersey, whom Nathan had met at the Western Wall in Jerusalem. When Nathan is slow in responding, Jimmy becomes insistent. Despite his rabbinical disguise he is planning to hijack the flight and seeks Nathan's help. He wants to force the Israeli government to close Yad Vashem, the Museum of the Holocaust in Jerusalem. The Jews, Lustig insists, must change their ways. They must stop reminding the world of the Holocaust. Only in the advocacy of "Forget Remembering" can they release the world (and themselves) from identifying the Jew as superego and conscience. Only by creating a new social movement for the obliteration of memory can they hope to extricate themselves from fulfilling the most difficult, painful function of human life.

The hijack attempt is thwarted by two Israeli security agents, who drag Jimmy and Nathan to the front of the plane. What mostly occupies them is the explanation of their own views, for they feel it necessary to refute Jimmy's arguments, which they have overheard. From their perspective Jimmy is completely wrong: it is not the Jewish superego the Gentiles hate but the Jewish assertion of the id. "The Holocaust should have taught them never to have an id *again*" (178).

UNDERSTANDING PHILIP ROTH

Throughout the novel Nathan is assaulted by contradictory interpretations of the same events. Different characters insist what that they have experienced is historically significant—and diametrically opposed to the views of others. Nathan encounters these different views and individuals at the moment of their presumed transformation into forces of history. They cease to be views or opinions put forward by individuals and become ideologies expounded in the name of history and destiny. The words they use change from everyday phrases into political slogans. Famed for his linguistic abilities, Nathan is the ear and eye and mouth each character seeks to dominate, so that only one story will be told. It is his vision each wants to influence, his book they all want to revise. Nathan thus becomes the ego function of the novel. He is the crossing point of its dialectical poles. Like Walt Whitman he contains them all—these multitudes of the modern American and Jewish imagination. And like Whitman he resists the pressure to unify and sanitize and present only one view. Nathan the writer, it turns out, is the one the security agents really want to hear their lecture. They are convinced that if they can convince him, he will spread their views. Like Jimmy, Henry, and Lippman's wife, they turn out to be American Jews who have emigrated to Israel and taken on new identities and roles there.

Once Nathan leaves Israel the novel again shifts gears. Now it is Nathan who must choose between impotence or, at the risk of death from heart surgery, marriage to Maria. Much of the fourth section, "Gloucester-shire," takes place in the Manhattan brownstone in which Nathan lives and works. Maria, seventeen years his junior, the mother of a young daughter, is living just upstairs, married to a British diplomat who doesn't love her. Maria and Nathan meet in the elevator. Passive, unaggressive, delicate, subtle and nuanced in her speech, and very "English," Maria is as charmed by Nathan's "exoticism" as he is by hers. For each the other is a counterlove, as different from former loves as they are from each other. Fearing he's written himself out of life after all those years spent "turning sentences around," Nathan opts for the surgery that will allow him to offer Maria (and himself) more than the afternoon conversations in his apartment which have thus far sustained their chaste passion for each other.

In the middle of this section Henry takes over the narration. Now it is Henry thinking about the eulogy he can't write for Nathan's funeral, rather than the other way around. The narrative describes Henry's thoughts and feelings without the mediation of Nathan the novelist to make Henry "more interesting." Or, as Henry would have it, without Nathan's distortions for the sake of his art. Not trusting Nathan's artistic discretion even from beyond the grave, Henry bribes Nathan's landlady to let him into Nathan's apartment. His worst fears are confirmed by what he finds there. Checking the shelf of Nathan's journals, Henry finds the one marked with the year of his affair with his Maria ten years before. Sure enough, everything he had told Nathan about that affair is there. The publication of Nathan's journals after his death could ruin Henry's marriage with Carol. But it takes Henry some time longer to realize that the journals are not the only danger. Nathan has already made use of the journal material in the draft of his current novel in progress—*The Counterlife*—so neatly arranged on his desk. Suddenly Henry feels justified for every ugly, resentful, unloving, unable-to-grieve thought he's had that day, and mentally castigates his dead brother for the misdeeds of Nathan the writer as well as his brotherly betrayal of him. Henry now sees (as Nathan has told Carol in "Judea") that brothers understand and experience each other as "deformation[s] of themselves." In the manuscript of the novel which Henry is reading, Nathan's

Henry is, if anyone, *him*—it's Nathan, using me to conceal himself while simultaneously disguising himself *as* himself, as *responsible*, as *sane*, disguising himself as a reasonable man while I am revealed as the absolute dope. . . . Nathan always wins. Fratricide without pain—a free ride. . . . *He*, not me, was the fool who died for a fuck, . . . who died the idiotic death of a fifteen-year-old, trying to get laid. *Dying* to get laid (226–27).

Henry reads through the manuscript of *The Counterlife*, from "Basel" through the "Judea," "Aloft," and "Gloucestershire" sections, which the reader has already perused, and comes to a section the reader has not yet encountered, "Christendom." Whose manuscript, then, is the real novel, Henry's or the reader's? Is *The Counterlife* Philip Roth's novel about the Zuckerman brothers or Nathan's? If Nathan's novel, then how can the reader be reading about Nathan's death? The last pages of "Gloucestershire" are an interview with Maria, though it is not clear to whom (Nathan or Nathan's ghost) she is speaking. Again, as with Henry, her voice is unmediated by Nathan's shaping or (depending on the reader's perspective) distorting artistry. And, like Henry, she takes the opportunity to offer her critique of Nathan's work, which becomes, self-reflexively, a critique of *The Counterlife*—specifically the piece she discovers in his apartment after his death entitled "Christendom."

Just as Henry sees Nathan's deforming use of him in "Basel" and "Judea" as a projection of Nathan's own distorted and distorting obsessions, so Maria, reading "Christendom," suspects that the hatred and disgust for Jews expressed there and attributed to her sister, Sarah, are really Nathan's own feelings about Christian women turned inside out. She believes they are Nathan's own doubts projected and expressed at a partial and only partially successful remove. Though part of the thick texture and rhetorical brilliance of *The Counterlife* derives from its inclusion of various and contradictory perspectives on issues ranging from Zionism to the writer's use, or distortion, of private material for his "narrative factory," for Henry and Maria, Nathan can only write about himself. Everything he writes is about "his kind of reality," yet "everything [is] reinvented," according to Maria, "even himself" (247, 250). Henry finishes his reading and leaves Nathan's apartment with the offending sections of the journals and novel, which he disposes of in a nearby garbage can.

In the concluding section of the novel, "Christendom," a suddenly quite alive Nathan tends to concur with the view of himself which Henry and Maria share, though Nathan places a different value upon it. Here Nathan the writer is someone exhausted by his arduously attained private culture and personal memories. His old habits and old quarrels with his critics and detractors can no longer provide him with new material for his work. He has come to England to find respite from his constant efforts. Having escaped Israel's intensities, he must be tested by its counterlife, England. Yet once there Nathan, like Roth, cannot leave well enough alone. On his return to England from Judea, from his "journey" to what Maria in a phrase with anti-Semitic overtones calls "the Jewish heart of darkness," his overt agenda is to don the mask of "Maria's husband." This role he believes will rejuvenate him. Seemingly happy and centered, Nathan is now occupied in renovating their dream house on the Thames. Suddenly, however, he begins to find signs of English anti-Semitism in his wife's family, in the English upper crust, and finally in his wife herself. In so doing, Nathan seems to be—

according to Maria—willfully destroying his chance at their English counterlife of beauty, peace, and pastoral simplicity.

Really listening to a Christmas service for the first time, Nathan discovers a profound revulsion. As though he'd never noticed it before, the virgin birth of Christ is suddenly "offensive kitsch"; the Nativity and the Resurrection nakedly address the most childish needs; and everyone in his immediate vicinity harbors anti-Semitic thoughts and sentiments of the darkest hue. As in *Portnoy's Complaint*, Roth on Christians and Christianity can be as devastating and as funny as Roth on Jews and Jewishness. But Roth is also pointing to the possibility that Nathan's reaction may be clear-eyed realism at last—or is it Jewish paranoia, the almost wistful readiness to see and hear anti-Semitism around every corner? Does the anti-Semitism in which English aristocratic culture is drenched really matter, Maria asks Nathan, or does he find it a chance to pick a fight by exaggerating differences? Confronting Maria's hostile and deeply anti-Semitic sister, Nathan admits that he has no unitary self: "I can only exhibit myself in disguise. All my audacity derives from masks" (275). Is his Jewishness only accidental then, a condition resulting from the effects of chance? Is life not fateful, as realistic novels argue, in the everyday details, but, like a modern novel, just a matter of perspective? If that is the case, then his identity is not single or singular but only a matter of which set of roles are played. Nathan claims that he has no real self but is only a performer impersonating different selves (320).

Nevertheless, Nathan is unable to believe in the pastoral counterlife he has worked so hard and undergone so much to create. The hollowness of the fantasy is revealed in the unexpected depths of his feelings regarding the conflict he foresees with Maria and her family over the circumcision of his as-yet unborn son (if the child turns out to be a male). As Nathan sees it, the reality of circumcision will bring his son out of the illusory English Garden of Eden.

Circumcision is startling, all right, particularly when performed by a garlicked old man upon the glory of a newborn body, but then maybe that's what the Jews had in mind and what makes the act seem quintessentially Jewish and the mark of their reality. Circumcision makes it clear as can be that you are here and not there, that you are out and not in—also that you're mine and not theirs. There is no way around it: you enter history through my history and me. Circumcision is everything that the pastoral is not and . . . reinforces what the world is about, which isn't strifeless unity (323).

Nathan chooses Jewishness over English pastoral, an active life over a passive one, thereby revealing the fundamental Jewishness of his vision of life. And in keeping with Nathan's pluralistic view of Jewish and American life—and here he differs from all earlier Roth protago-

nists—one counterlife does not and cannot replace another. Rather, they all coexist simultaneously. For him
the open-ended and rich limbo of polarized potentialities, which has haunted Roth's potent/impotent Jewish
sons all along, is infinitely preferable to the closing off
of any part of the spectrum of life's possibilities:

The burden isn't either/or, consciously choosing from
possibilities equally difficult and regrettable—it's and/
and/and/and/and as well. Life *is* and: the accidental and
the immutable, the elusive and the graspable, the bizarre and the predictable, the actual and the potential,
all the multiplying realities, entangled, overlapping,
colliding, conjoined—plus the multiplying illusions!
This times this times this times this . . . (306).

The novel's hall of mirrors affirms the power of the
imagination and celebrates the multiple possibilities of
life rather than its singular certainties. Despite their
agonies of self-doubt and self-laceration, despite their
angst and their regrets, Roth's protagonists are right
where they want to be: in the thick of it, with all life's
rich potentialities and counterlives still before them. If
this sounds like perpetual sonship (and to Henry it
does), it is one resolution to the nexus of Jewishness
and masculinity. "Alienated both from claustrophobic
Jewishness and vertiginous Americanness" and from
their Zionistic and their skeptical counterparts in Israel,
Roth's protagonists, "hellenized—hedonized—egoma-

niazed" American Jews must "reinvent" themselves.[7] Like the protagonists of *The Counterlife*, they must open-endedly appropriate and project counterlives as best they can. Henry, the New Jersey dentist obsessed by oral sex and reborn Zionist; Nathan, the Jewish comic performer and American writer; Lustig, the gleeful baseball player and hijacker disguised as a Hasidic rabbi; Lippman, the American exile and Jewish man of action; Shuki, the cynical intellectual and committed Jewish patriot—all are part of Nathan's own bewildering set of possibilities. Roth here redefines conventional notions of failure and success, for in a world where each Jew contains multiple personalities like a Hebraicized version of Walt Whitman's motto "I contain multitudes," clarity and self-definition can only be contingent and momentary.

In *The Ghost Writer* Zuckerman tells Lonoff that the Jewish writer is an intellectual with "blood in his penis." *The Counterlife* takes this statement as its implicit starting point and transforms it from a private statement into a question of public definition. A meditation on the relationship of impotence and vision, *The Counterlife* is about the possibility of re-vision—the writer revising his work, the character revising his life, a people recreating their national life. As Maria notes of Zuckerman in her imagined interview, "He said to me, 'A time comes when you have to forget what frightens you most.' But I don't think it was dying that most frightened him—it was facing the impotence for the rest of his life" (246).

This urge for the fullness of life, revealed in the final paragraph of the novel, in which Nathan is no longer impotent but erect, blurs the boundaries between fantasy and reality. "How does one know what is real or false with a writer like that?" Maria wonders (247). Part of the thickness and social density of *The Counterlife* comes from its strategy of repetition and variation; what for Shuki is Nathan's ironic gift is for Henry "the comic hyperbole insidiously undermining everything it chose to touch" (205). Many points of view are included that present various, even conflicting perspectives on the same issue or topic. The result is to create what the Irish poet Yeats called the "emotion of multitude,"[8] as if many people were experiencing the same overlapping events. This is not something that happens to a single individual; these historical moments determine the lives of an entire people. Nathan has brought Maria to question her privileged reality. Her phrase calls to mind the motto with which Herzl founded modern Zionism: *Im tirzu eyn zo agada*—if you wish it, it is not a dream—leading to the recreation of modern Jewish life and the founding of the modern state of Israel.

Like all the other extravagant and exuberant Jewish characters in this novel, Nathan is a Jew by reason "of imagination."[9] *The Counterlife,* like the earlier great Roth tales, especially *Goodbye, Columbus, Portnoy's Complaint,* and *The Ghost Writer,* is about the exercise of the imagination to remake the self, family, and nation and open it to the range of possibility. The novel dramatizes the urge to experience contradiction and accept its necessity by rendering an astounding gallery of characters, each of whom persuades the reader to believe in his or her reality by the force of his or her words. And in Roth's novels it is in talk that the imagination makes its pressure felt. Over and over again Roth demonstrates that he has an unerring ear for colloquial speech: the many-sided arguments are swiftly and convincingly presented, each faction speaking in precisely its own rhetoric. His prose is as vivid and as immediate as film images. Visual and auditory elements combine to produce an immediate experience. Quotation will not suffice; turn, for example, to the section in "Judea" where Nathan approaches the Western Wall of the Second Temple, and note the ways in which each voice is given its unique qualities, yet all together they create a fugue. This is brilliant "thick description,"[10] in which the novel recaptures its potential as a comic epic.

Roth's imagination reveals the power that creates lives and counterlives. This is also the surprising power of humor—of the joke that with its punch line reverses everything and turns the tables on the pessimist. Its vivid accents echo in Henry's memory of a student questioning Nathan, asking

if he wrote "in quest of immortality." He could hear Nathan laughing and giving the answer. . . . "If you're from New Jersey," Nathan had said, "and you write thirty books and you win the Nobel Prize, and you live to be white-haired and ninety-five, it's highly unlikely but not impossible that after your death they'll decide to name a rest stop for you on the Jersey Turnpike. And so, long after you're gone, you may indeed be remembered, but mostly by small children, in the backs of cars, when they lean forward and tell their parents, 'Stop, please, stop at Zuckerman—I have to make a pee.' For a New Jersey novelist that's as much immortality as it's realistic to hope for" (237).

Here too, as everywhere else in this novel, the perspectives that define what is real are multiple, and our comic laughter acknowledges their irreducible pluralism.

Notes

1. See Mikhail Bakhtin, *The Dialogic Imagination,* ed. Michael Holquist (Austin: University of Texas Press, 1981).

2. Roth, *The Counterlife* (New York: Farrar, Straus, 1987) 37. Further references will be noted parenthetically.

3. Julian Barnes, "Philip Roth in Israel: *The Counterlife,*" *London Review of Books* 5 (5 Mar. 1987): 3.

4. Barnes 3.

5. Roth reported on this dialogue in "Second Dialogue in Israel," *Reading Myself and Others.*

6. This episode of *The Counterlife* echoes the concluding section of D. M. Thomas's powerful *White Hotel,* where all its Jewish characters, after having been killed by the Nazis, come back to a redeemed life in the land of Israel.

7. Hermione Lee, *Philip Roth* (New York: Methuen, 1982) 45.

8. William Butler Yeats, *Essays and Introductions* (New York: Macmillan, 1961) 215–16.

9. Jacob Neusner, *American Jewry and the Arts: We Are Jews by Reason of Imagination* (New York: National Foundation for Jewish Culture, 1987). This was the keynote address for the conference on Art and Identity in the American Jewish Community, Los Angeles, 18 Jan. 1987.

10. The phrase is Clifford Geertz's and refers to the ability to capture an entire cultural moment; see his "Thick Description: Toward an Interpretive Theory of Culture," *The Interpretation of Cultures* (New York: Basic Books, 1973).

CHAPTER NINE

Editing Himself and Others: Criticism and Autobiography

After publishing his two major political satires, *Our Gang* in 1971 and *The Great American Novel* in 1973, Roth turned to Eastern Europe to explore the reciprocal relationship of politics and culture. He wrote the important essay "'I Always Wanted You to Admire My Fasting': or, Looking at Kafka,"[1] and in 1974 he became general editor of the Penguin Books series "Writers from the Other Europe." Thus far fifteen books, among them the most distinguished Eastern European fiction written since World War II, have been published in this series. Roth has written introductions to two of the volumes, Milan Kundera's *Laughable Loves* and *The Book of Laughter and Forgetting*.

In his preface Roth states that the purpose of this series

is to bring together outstanding and influential works of fiction by Eastern European writers. In many instances they will be writers who, though recognized as powerful forces in their own cultures, are virtually un-

known in the West. It is hoped that by reprinting se-
lected Eastern European writers in this format and with
introductions that place each work in its literary and
historical context, the literature that has evolved in "the
other Europe," particularly during the postwar decades,
will be made more accessible to a new readership.

Focusing on the destruction of Eastern Europe during
World War II, highlighting the impact of the Holocaust
and the problem of reconstruction of a now culturally
homogenous area previously noted for its pluricultural
and multiethnic landscape, these "writers from the
Other Europe" have introduced the perspectives of the
victims of modern European history into the accounts
of the victors. Their new subjects have also had complex
literary treatments. Many of the novels in this series
combine unlikely genres and renew earlier literary traditions, especially surrealism. In making modern Eastern
European literature available to the general American
public, this series has changed its apprehension of the
European cultural map.

Reading Myself and Others (1975)

Roth's critical prose is deft and engaging, and as
surefooted as his fiction. Characters, themes, and subjects central to his fiction find a complex analytic treatment in the essays included in *Reading Myself and Others*.

EDITING HIMSELF AND OTHERS

All of them reflect Roth's concern to ground his work in the actual conditions of contemporary life. As a realistic writer he draws upon news reports, political events, and mundane situations. As a satirist Roth does not divide reality into deep and surface structure, but takes the face of everyday life as his point of departure. Just as his fiction inquires into the relationship between character and language, so in these essays he investigates the range of meanings implicated in the words people use to define and describe their experiences.

Throughout his work Roth emphasizes the impact of World War II on his generation. What he calls our "violent century" has entered even his earliest fiction, figuring prominently in two of the stories of *Goodbye, Columbus*, "Defender of the Faith" and "Eli, the Fanatic." Just as these stories explore the situation of the Jews in modern American and Western culture, so his essays elaborate their reciprocal impact. Like his stories these essays have a polemic edge, as he defends against simplifying and reductive views.

In 1975 Roth collected the twenty-three pieces he included in *Reading Myself and Others*, most of which had been previously published, as a way of gaining perspective on what he had been reading and writing since his first book of fiction appeared in 1959. "Because recognition—and with it, opposition—came to me almost immediately," he notes, "I . . . felt called upon both to assert a literary position and to defend my moral flank."[2] Since he has never regularly kept a diary or journal, these essays serve to record his thinking and reflections while writing fiction; they chart the "difficulties, enthusiasms, and aversions that have evolved along with my work" (xii).

The essays are informed by Roth's sense that "to the writer the community is, properly, both subject and audience" (134). Given this assumption, his community both provides the subject matter of his work—character, plot, and theme—and serves as the object of his criticism. Writing from and for his community, Roth also must stand apart from it. As an artist he needs the solitude that will make it possible for him to discover the ways in which the individual life both participates in communal values and yet is different from it. The inspiration for his writing is rooted in the talk he and his friends engaged in. Their neighborhood bull sessions "were the means by which we either took vengeance or tried to hold at bay the cultural forces that were shaping us." It was something, Roth notes, "like the folk narrative of a tribe passing from one stage of human development to the next." An "amalgam of mimicry, reporting, kibitzing, disputation, satire, and legendizing from which we drew so much sustenance," this rich mixture and complex discourse became his central allegiance (4–5).

When Roth satirizes life in the suburbs, he is matching alienated suburban behavior against the camaraderie of his boyhood. The political manipulations of language are underscored by their differences from this elaborate communal talk in which the fullness of his and his friends' personalities were embodied. Their conversation—what ethnicity is all about—expresses the primary connections against which the secondary relationships of the dispersed suburban world are to be measured. Growing out of his reflections on the meaning and power of those primary relationships and their rich discourse, these essays define the conditions for contemporary satire.

Part 1 of *Reading Myself and Others* includes ten interviews and comments on his own novels grouped around the theme of "reading myself." They reveal a most perceptive critic discussing and justifying his own work and moral vision. The first piece "Writing and the Powers That Be," is an interview conducted by an Italian critic about writers and power. Roth refuses to provide simple answers to the interviewer's leading questions. He notes that while the coercive forces of family and religion have been a recurrent subject in his fiction, from *Goodbye, Columbus* to *Portnoy's Complaint* and *Our Gang*, unlike the interviewer who assumes "family and religion as power and nothing else," Roth believes they are much more complicated phenomena. He has, he comments, subjected these "connections to considerable scrutiny." Ozzie Freedman, Alexander Portnoy, and Lucy Nelson are all characters expressing their anger against those who have misused their power (8, 9). By contrast, Roth concludes, "whatever serious acts of rebelliousness I may have engaged in as a novelist have been directed far more at my own imagination's system of constraints and habits of expression than at the powers that vie for control in the world" (13).

Roth continues his habit of scrutinizing his loyalties in the next piece, an interview conducted by George Plimpton entitled "On *Portnoy's Complaint*." In it he makes an important comment about the influence of Kafka on the genesis of *Portnoy*. Rather than Lenny Bruce, Mort Sahl, Shelley Berman, or other Jewish stand-up comics, it was Kafka's work, which he encountered while teaching at the University of Pennsylvania, that made it possible for Roth to grasp the central thread of *Portnoy*: guilt as a comic idea. His reflections upon modern literature thus led him to develop not only the manic-monologue narrative strategy of the novel but also the links between psychological processes and the desperation of the comic performer. Roth is careful to emphasize that it is his *thinking*, not the events of his life, that led him to his breakthrough in his writing. Thus in the next essay Roth responds in careful detail to Diana Trilling's charges that he has a "showy literary manner" and "achieves his effects by the broadest possible strokes" (25). Trilling's efforts to discredit his literary ability lead Roth to a penetrating discussion of the moral discriminations, ironies, and literary technique of *When She Was Good* and *Portnoy's Complaint*. Diana Trilling is mistaken in identifying Roth, the writer, with Portnoy, the narrator. "May I suggest," Roth concludes, that the writer's "view of life is more hidden from certain readers, . . . more embedded in parody, burlesque, slapstick, ridicule, insult, invective, lampoon, wisecrack, in nonsense, in levity, in *play*—in, that is, the methods and devices of Comedy, than their own view of life may enable them to realize" (30–31).

In "On *The Breast*," Roth discusses how much of his work has been about men and women living "beyond their psychological and moral means." Their extreme behavior sweeps them "out to sea, sometimes on a tide of their own righteousness or resentment" (65). His discussion reveals the program behind his novels—to encompass the range of the American family by analyzing its polar opposites. Lucy Nelson and Alexander Portnoy "are two very stubborn American children," he notes, "locked in prototypical combat with the beloved enemy: the spirited Jewish boy pitted against his mother, the Cleopatra of the kitchen; the solemn Gentile girl pitted against her father, the Bacchus of Hometown, U.S.A." Neither of them succeeds in escaping from the defining familial situation. By contrast with both of them David Kepesh, the protagonist of *The Breast*, "strikes me as far more heroic than either of these two: perhaps a man who turns into a breast is the first heroic character I've ever been able to portray" (66). Roth then goes on to emphasize how the power of this novel resides in the simultaneous transparency and opacity of its central image.

"On *The Great American Novel*" an interview which Roth conducted with himself to carry forward his discussion of satire and comedy, differentiates their power in this book from that of earlier ones, including *Our Gang*. The essay, an important response to his critics, leads Roth to use Philip Rahv's fundamental distinction between the American writer as paleface or as redskin. What Rahv has divided Roth fuses: it is Roth as "redface" who brings together the emotional and spontaneous qualities of the redskin and the moral discriminations of the paleface. Baseball, the Bible, American political culture in both its high and low cultural manifestations, classic American literary traditions and the habits of the American comic strip join in *The Great American Novel*; it is an effort to chart the imagining of American reality by the redface.

Part 2 of *Reading Myself and Others* focuses on more general questions, which are dealt with by recourse to specific instances and factual detail. As in the earlier essays Roth's insights derive from his own fictional practice, but here he broadens their reach. In the first essay, "Writing American Fiction," Roth probes the meanings of a Chicago newspaper story concerning the disappearance of two teen-age girls. "And what is the moral of the story? Simply this": that the American writer "in the middle of the twentieth century has his hands full in trying to understand, describe, and then make *credible* much of American reality." American culture "tosses up figures almost daily that are the envy of any novelist" (120). How then is the writer to deal with a reality that constantly outdoes fiction? One strategy,

EDITING HIMSELF AND OTHERS

Roth comments, is to escape from realism into the abstract myth that characterizes the writing of Bernard Malamud. Another is to emphasize the personality of the writer, as Norman Mailer does, instead of the world he is supposedly creating. Ralph Ellison's strategy, which Roth values more highly, is to draw upon a communal subject matter and speak to a communal audience.

"Some New Jewish Stereotypes" carries forward the previous discussion of the need for a realistic fiction by taking issue with the stereotypes of Jews in the work of Harry Golden and Leon Uris. Then, in "Writing About Jews," Roth tries to account for the animosity his writing has provoked among many of his Jewish readers. Responding to some of the letters he received after the publication of *Goodbye, Columbus,* he provides a definition of the function of fiction:

Fiction is not written to affirm the principles and beliefs that everybody seems to hold, nor does it seek to guarantee the appropriateness of our feelings. The world of fiction, in fact, frees us from the circumscription that society places upon feeling; one of the greatnesses of the art is that it allows both the writer and the reader to respond to experience in ways not always available in day-to-day conduct. . . . We may not even know that we have such a range of feelings and responses *until* we have come into contact with the work of fiction (151).

As a perspectival writer Roth does not give "reality" pride of place; no one account has greater authority by virtue of matching the way things are. Rather, stories reveal that there are various ways things are; in Roth's view this kind of fiction makes the pluralism of realities available, thus freeing the reader to discover ranges of feeling repressed by the prevailing social order.

"Imagining the Erotic: Three Introductions" continues Roth's exploration of the surreal unreality of the modern world by means of careful discussion of novels by Alan Lelchuk, Milan Kundera, and Fredrica Wagman. This theme is further analyzed in the last section of this book, " 'I Always Wanted You to Admire My Fasting'; or, Looking at Kafka"—the writer who has had perhaps the most profound and lasting influence on Roth's work. In this essay, which is also in part a fictional narrative, Roth presents a sustained meditation on Kafka's life and work, which reveals both how important it is to read it with care and how such a reading can lead to the most imaginative speculation. What, he asks, would it have been like had Kafka not died in 1924 but managed to get to the United States in 1942? While his three sisters were in fact killed by the Nazis, this imaginary Kafka makes it to New Jersey and becomes the nine-year-old Roth's Hebrew teacher. To this young boy and his friends he is not Dr. Kafka but Dr. Kishka— the Yiddish word for intestines and a kind of sausage. Whatever his name, Philip Roth's lonely teacher is

EDITING HIMSELF AND OTHERS

asked to Sabbath dinner one Friday night. There he is introduced to Aunt Rhoda, his mother's unmarried sister. Though both aunt and teacher are awkward and shy, a friendship does develop between them. However, just as the romance seems about to blossom into marriage, a catastrophe occurs when the two go away for a weekend in Atlantic City. The fictional Roth and his brother speculate that it is sex that has ruined everything. Later, when he is in college, his mother sends him an obituary notice for his Hebrew teacher, clipped from the newspaper. All traces of this Kafka's work have disappeared, and the great novels and stories are not left to posterity. Roth concludes his meditation by returning to Kafka's story "The Hunger Artist," from which he has quoted an epigraph and taken the title of his own essay. He leaves the reader wondering which destiny—life as a bachelor in New Jersey or that of the desperate Prague writer—is more appropriate to the surreal real Kafka.

Reading Myself and Others is dedicated to Saul Bellow—"the 'other' I have read from the beginning with the deepest pleasure and admiration." The book as a whole reveals the seriousness with which Roth takes his profession as a writer and the cultural importance with which he invests his subjects. It is a fitting tribute to Bellow, who led the way and made it possible for other American writers to engage the modern condition as intellectuals.

UNDERSTANDING PHILIP ROTH

A Philip Roth Reader (1980)

In 1980, after twenty years of writing, Roth edited *A Philip Roth Reader*. The arrangement and the selections he included reveal his understanding of the range of his work. The detailed outline of many of the excerpts which he provides read as if they were derived from Roth's working notes, offering a glimpse into the process of his fictional production. In his introduction to the volume the novelist Martin Green notes that the episodes in the first section focus on the literary context of Roth's work; the second part presents that aspect which has made him most famous—"the wild extravaganza upon the theme of a serious moral dilemma"; and the third section "reminds us of the process of self-indictment which lies at the root of everything else in Roth." Green's insights direct us to the extent and variety of Roth's achievement by focusing on the areas of the Jewish psyche and the American social situation which he has mapped more fully than any of his contemporaries. The title of each section of the collection is in the form of a personal comment and is placed in quotation marks. The first two are colloquial, the third an imperative command. Each functions to define an individual whose crises and problems are defined by the excerpts included in that section. The notes Roth provides have the quality of stage directions. Thus they suggest the characteristic visual and auditory effects of the monologue of one of his characters.

EDITING HIMSELF AND OTHERS

Part 1, entitled, "Literature Got Me into This and Literature Is Gonna Have to Get Me Out," includes five selections. Subheadings and brief synopses, presumably done by Roth himself, point out the central themes. Throughout, marriage as a literary convention is central. Roth emphasizes the analogy between the commitments of love and the marriage bed and the commitments of the artist to his art. "Literature" thus not only comes to denote the world of books but also becomes a metaphor for the seductions of marriage—and vice versa, as marriage becomes a metaphor for the seductions of literature. Having gotten the Rothian character "into this," literature will have to get him out—not only of the difficulties of the intellectual life but the troubles of marriage as well. It follows then that these selections serve as models of and for both sets of problems. There is also the implication that they may also have therapeutic power.

Part 2 is entitled "Only It Ain't No Joke!" As we read through these selections, "it" comes to refer to politics and the manipulation of people through the use of political rhetoric. Ironically, victory in these excerpts turns out at times to be worse than defeat, even for the hapless baseball team the Mundys and Portnoy with his masturbatory pyrotechnics. What these selections all have in common is their fullness of description, a method characteristic of Roth which is used dramatically to hide rather than reveal the true situation.

Part 3 is entitled "You Must Change Your Life." In

all the excerpts the characters must change their lives in order to learn how to live with painful situations that cannot be resolved. In this way the selections prepare for the reading of *The Breast*, with which this section concludes and which details how David Kepesh learns to live his life once he has been transformed into a giant mammary gland with a five-inch nipple. "Novotny's Pain," a tale that describes the developing back pain of a young soldier who has been drafted into the army in the early months of the Korean War, is the first piece. Next comes "Martha's Thanksgiving," an excerpt from *Letting Go*, set near the University of Chicago in the middle of the 1950s. In "Cynthia's New Life," also from *Letting Go*, Martha's children, Cynthia and Mark, have left Chicago "to live with their father and his new wife in the East. Martha, their mother has let them go, hoping a new life will be better for all, and knowing just what an illusion a new life can be."[3] In the next piece Roth characterizes "Lucy's Will," from part 2 of *When She Was Good*, in the following terms:

The time is 1949, in the Middle West. The characters are Lucy Nelson, who has grown up most unhappily in Liberty Center, and sees in Fort Kean College for Women her first real haven from the humiliations of being the daughter of an alcoholic father (Duane "Whitey" Nelson) and a defenseless mother (Myra); Roy Bassart, a young ex-G.I., just entering a Fort Kean photography school, and the hometown beau whom

Lucy had also hoped to escape at college; Daddy Will Caroll, her mother's father, with whom the Nelsons have had to live since Lucy's early childhood; Roy's father, Lloyd Bassart, a high-school teacher in Liberty Center; and Roy's favorite uncle, Julian Sowerby, a Liberty Center businessman, who for a time looked to Lucy to have the manly know-how lacking in a Whitey Nelson, or a Roy Bassart (345).

This full outline of the novel suggests the grimness of the situation Lucy cannot escape. It prepares by contrast for "Chez Claire," the closing section of *The Professor of Desire*, which describes the reconciliation of David Kepesh with his father as well as his father's acceptance of Herbert Barbatnik, a friend and Holocaust survivor. Claire, David's lover, makes these rapprochements possible by helping him acknowledge and defuse his anger. *A Philip Roth Reader* concludes with the complete text of *The Breast*, which ends with the last line of the Rilke poem that gives its name to this section of the *Reader*, "You must change your life." In ending with this statement Roth implies that the realities which he evokes in his work make a similar demand. As the mythic power of the god Apollo in Rilke's poem sweeps the viewer to a new understanding of his situation, so will Roth's work, which puts the modern reader in touch with the fundamental experiences of life. Art *does* redeem—if we are attuned to it. The imperative mood of the statement—the "must" in the last line—however, makes it clear that such redemption can only come if we hearken to art, to literature, like a religious participant in its rites.

The Facts: A Novelist's Autobiography (1988)

In *The Facts: A Novelist's Autobiography*, Roth presents his own life, like that of many characters in his novels, as if it were a *Bildungsroman* of a young man's education. The protagonist of Roth's autobiography is the artist-to-be progressing from life in the family, through schooling in college and postgraduate degrees, to the discovery of his role as a writer, lover, husband, and intellectual. In this pattern the increase of knowledge and experience leads to the embrace not of harmonious wisdom but of a polemic stance: in growing up and responding to the demands of the various institutions he must deal with, Roth progressively extricates himself from them. He repudiates the entanglements of all institutions and conventional habits. Increasingly, he confronts the blunt facts of life directly, calling the manifold mediations of everyday life that disguise the facts to our attention as a way of discrediting their ideological power.

The Facts begins with an apologetic letter from Roth to Nathan Zuckerman, describing the problems he has had in writing his autobiography. He notes that in all his previous work the imaginative event began with the specific facts; to make the facts the conclusion of the process of his writing, as he has done here, is to make this autobiography a book written "absolutely backward." Instead of springing from the facts into fiction, Roth has taken "what I have already imagined" and, "desiccating it," has tried to restore his experience to the "original, prefictionalized factuality."[4] The use of phrases like *prefictionalized factuality* and words like *desiccating* suggest the difficulties involved in moving from the finished work back to its factual sources.

Once the issue has been conceptualized, however, Roth's prose settles into its deft and engaging style. His voice becomes increasingly persuasive as he asks Zuckerman whether he should publish this manuscript in which he is presented undisguised. He does admit that after a prolonged physical and mental ordeal growing out of what was expected to be only minor surgery, it has taken an unusual effort to write the autobiography; he has, however, persisted in order to recover a sense of himself that he had lost. In that effort of recovery, which turns out to encompass many roles, "I found no one moment of origin but a series of moments, a history of multiple origins" (5).

With this idea Roth raises complex issues about the nature of personality and identity. They echo the questions he has raised about many of his characters, even though he has been careful to emphasize the differences between the fictional enterprise and this factual manuscript. In the interest of recovering those "real-life" origins, Roth has avoided the temptation to dramatize "untruthfully the insufficiently dramatic, to complicate the essentially simple, to charge with implication what implied very little," and not abandon the facts for fiction. The result, he states, is a manuscript which embodies "*my* counterlife." Having relinquished his disguises and different roles, this autobiography, by contrast with *The Counterlife*, which "can be read as fiction about structure," is "the bare bones, the structure of a life without the fiction" (6).

The same comparison serves as an epigraph to *The Facts*, in the form of a quotation from Nathan Zuckerman's thoughts in *The Counterlife*: "And as he spoke I was thinking, *the kind of stories that people turn life into, the kind of lives that people turn stories into.*" Zuckerman's comment reveals the equation Roth has made explicit in this narrative. Autobiography and fiction meet at the point where facts encounter narration. This point at which lives and stories meet is the moment of crisis. Each of the chapters centers on one such moment, with the book as a whole bracketed at beginning and end by references to the ordeal of surgery that led him to the edge of "emotional and mental dissolution" (5). Echoing *The Anatomy Lesson*, physical pain and the urgent presence of death have led Roth to reconsider the process of self-transformation of his fiction, and thus to dwell upon the facts.

The autobiography ends with a long letter from Nathan Zuckerman to Roth telling him not to publish:

EDITING HIMSELF AND OTHERS

"You are far better off writing about me than 'accurately' reporting your own life" (161). Nathan claims that by leaving out the imagination, Roth has written an inaccurate account. In fact, what he has done has not presented the real "'you'" but Roth as "what you want to look like to your readers at the age of fifty-five" (164). The facts, Zuckerman claims, just don't add up to much; Roth would have been better off writing about Nathan's life. Reality, Nathan insists, cannot compete with fiction. At this point other central characters of *The Counterlife* enter Roth's autobiography, stepping out of their fictional frame. For as Nathan says, while Roth has been working on his autobiography, Nathan has grown a beard, and now his wife Maria, in her eighth month of pregnancy, claims he did it to look Jewish and ruin their pastoral idyll in England. Nathan accuses Roth of having prepared a shattering conflict for them just when he is delighting in the "'beautiful'" existence Maria has been making for him.

Nathan's role in the autobiography echoes that of Don Quixote in the second part of Cervantes' novel. Both appear to have an existence independent of their author; both question the writer as to why he has given them particular roles to play and challenge that decision; and both claim the need for change and autonomous independence. To have Nathan playing such a role in an autobiography, however, lends added weight to his charge that Roth is writing an unconscious work of fiction. As further evidence Nathan asks why Roth hasn't used his now-dead wife's real name. Would it be because then in the world of imagination she would have had the right to answer his account of her aggressive behavior toward him? Since the last three chapters all focus on her, describing first how Roth pursued her and, entering into a relationship with her which quickly turned sour, tried to extricate himself from it, only to be tricked into marriage and was then forced to live in its hellish reality, Nathan's charge must be taken seriously. Nathan is claiming that Roth's emphasis on the facts cannot endow his account with the authority of the omniscient narrator of the realistic novel; there is no escape from the perspectivist's world. There is no external standpoint from which to pass judgment here; as in so much of Roth's work what must be done is to inspect and evaluate the surface of the narrative and the social world. The reality of each of the many points of view must be conceded. Each generates a story in which all the others are implicated.

Five situations are central to the autobiography, and they echo Roth's fictional practice. First of all, there is the relationship of father and son, with the son fulfilling in an ironic way the father's dreams, thereby becoming a hero of his community. Then the narrative focuses on the young Jew as emergent sexual intellectual, analyzing the nexus of eros and thought as part of growing up and going to college. This leads to a playing out of the connection of the theatrical qualities of modern Jewish life to Roth's personal sense of power and exuber-

ance. The guilt of marriage, and the war between part-
ners in it, comes forward next, as we learn that large
sections of *My Life as a Man*, including how Peter Tarnopol was tricked into marriage by Maureen Mezik
Johnson, closely follow the facts of Roth's experience.
Roth's response to the attack on his work mounted by
segments of the organized Jewish community parallels
his experiences in his disastrous marriage; together both
lead him to the desire to free himself from all entangling
alliances. Throughout, much of the prose reads like an
interview. Roth's skill at interviewing fellow writers like
Primo Levi and Aharon Appelfeld, revealing how life
and work intertwine, is here applied to himself to discover how his skills as a human being and a writer have
saved him from catastrophe.

Against the facts which Roth brings forward, the
title of the book and several of its chapters—"Joe College," "Girl of My Dreams," and "All in the Family"—
echo the radio and television shows of popular culture.
As works of the popular imagination they echo the conventional lives, the stereotypes, against which Roth
places his own account. Each chapter's content, however, works against its title in an ironic way, beginning
with "Safe at Home," which is at once a baseball reference, an implicit comment on the safety Roth and his
family felt in America by contrast with World War II and
the murder of the Jews in Europe, and a way of highlighting by contrast the impact of the incursions of anti-
Semitism into their Newark neighborhood. Similarly,

the book's title serves to parody the world of *Dragnet*, Jack Webb's radio and television show in which the detective asks in each episode for "just the facts." This phrase prepares for their comic version in Roth's autobiographical enterprise.

The comic tone is also a way of responding to the central facts of this narrative, all of which deal with physical pain. Not only does the autobiography have its genesis in Roth's painful postoperative ordeal; his father is racked by terminal cancer, the Holocaust and World War II are present as painful experiences; and growing up in Newark, Roth has encountered the violence of anti-Semitism. Pain and the possibility of death are everywhere in the autobiography, as even Nathan cries out against the possibility that his creator will destroy him. This comedy thus is not an evasion but a preparation for the difficulties of life.

In a recent interview Roth compares his relationship with Nathan Zuckerman to that of Edgar Bergen and his dummy, Charlie McCarthy.

Zuckerman's abiding function is to be . . . [my] front man. . . . The tradition in ventriloquism is that the dummy is always smarter than the ventriloquist; the joke is to have the dummy always being critical of the ventriloquist. Zuckerman is my dummy. He shows off for me, he challenges me. He's my creature, but that makes him all the more audacious.

EDITING HIMSELF AND OTHERS

Similarly, Roth reminds his readers that "I'm not going to pretend that I'm Portnoy. Why should I? Writing is a performance."[5]

Roth entitles the last chapter of his own narrative "Now vee may perhaps to begin," quoting the last line of *Portnoy's Complaint*. The phrase moves the narrative out of popular American conventions and institutions into the world of his own fictional creation. In the German-immigrant accents of Dr. Spielvogel, Jewish interpreter of dreams and fantasies, this chapter title refers to the process of psychoanalysis. Thereby it signals that Roth is no longer only "the personificator" (161) that Nathan wants him to be, but a cultural analyst and force, revealing the deepest structures of the modern condition. And as he reshapes language through his satire, Roth brings the experience of the Jew as intellectual and sexual being into the mythological world of American culture, reminding us that their encounter is at the heart of his comic universe.

Notes

1. " 'I Always Wanted You to Admire My Fasting': or, Looking at Kafka," was published in the *American Review* 17 (1973): 103–26, and included as the final piece in *Reading Myself and Others*.

2. Roth, *Reading Myself and Others* (New York: Farrar, Straus, 1975) xi. Further references will be noted parenthetically.

UNDERSTANDING PHILIP ROTH

3. Roth, *A Philip Roth Reader* (New York: Farrar, Straus, 1980) 323. Further references will be noted parenthetically.

4. Roth, *The Facts: A Novelist's Autobiography* (New York: Farrar, Straus, 1988) 3. Further references will be noted parenthetically.

5. "Philip Roth Faces *The Facts*," interview by Linda Matchan, *Boston Globe* 4 Oct. 1988: Sec. 3, 65.

BIBLIOGRAPHY

Works by Philip Roth
Books

Goodbye, Columbus. Boston: Houghton Mifflin, 1959; London: Andre Deutsch, 1959.

Letting Go. New York: Random House, 1962; London: Andre Deutsch, 1962.

When She Was Good. New York: Random House, 1967; London: Jonathan Cape. 1967.

Portnoy's Complaint. New York: Random House, 1969; London: Jonathan Cape, 1969.

Our Gang (Starring Tricky and His Friends). New York: Random House, 1971; London: Jonathan Cape, 1971.

The Breast. New York: Holt, Rinehart, 1972; London: Jonathan Cape, 1973.

The Great American Novel. New York: Holt, Rinehart, 1973; London: Jonathan Cape, 1973.

My Life as a Man. New York: Holt, Rinehart, 1974; London: Jonathan Cape, 1974.

Reading Myself and Others. New York: Farrar, Straus, 1975; London: Jonathan Cape, 1975.

The Professor of Desire. New York: Farrar, Straus, 1977; London: Jonathan Cape, 1978.

The Ghost Writer. New York: Farrar, Straus, 1979; London: Jonathan Cape, 1979.

A Philip Roth Reader. New York: Farrar, Straus, 1980; London: Jonathan Cape, 1980.

Zuckerman Unbound. New York: Farrar, Straus, 1981; London: Jonathan Cape, 1981.

The Anatomy Lesson. New York: Farrar, Straus, 1983; London: Jonathan Cape, 1984.

The Prague Orgy. London: Jonathan Cape, 1985.

Zuckerman Bound (includes *The Prague Orgy*). New York: Farrar, Straus, 1985.

257

BIBLIOGRAPHY

The Counterlife. New York: Farrar, Straus, 1987; London: Jonathan Cape, 1987.

The Facts: A Novelist's Autobiography. New York: Farrar, Straus, 1988; London: Jonathan Cape, 1988.

Uncollected Stories

"The Day It Snowed." *Chicago Review* 8 (1954): 34–45.

"The Contest for Aaron Gold." *Epoch* 5–6 (1955): 37–50.

"Heard Melodies Are Sweeter." *Esquire* Aug. 1958: 58.

"Expect the Vandals." *Esquire* Dec. 1958: 208–28.

"The Love Vessel." *Dial I* 1 (1959): 41–68.

"The Mistaken." *American Judaism* 10 (1960): 10.

"Psychoanalytic Special." *Esquire* Nov. 1963: 106.

"On the Air." *New American Review* 10 (1970): 7–49.

Uncollected Reviews

"Rescue from Philosophy." *New Republic* 10 June 1957: 22. On the film *Funny Face*.

"I Don't Want to Embarrass You." *New Republic* 15 July 1957: 21–22. On Edward R. Murrow's *Person to Person*.

"The Hurdles of Satire." *New Republic* 9 Sept. 1957: 22. On Sid Caesar's comedy hour.

"Coronation on Channel Two." *New Republic* 23 Sept. 1957: 21. On the Miss America Pageant.

"Films as Sociology." *New Republic* 21 Oct. 1957: 21–22. On the films *Something of Value* and *Hatful of Rain*.

"The Proper Study of Show Business." *New Republic* 23 Dec. 1957: 21. On the films *Pal Joey* and *Les Girls*.

"Channel X: Two Plays on the Race Conflict." *New York Review of Books* 28 May 1964: 10–13. On James Baldwin's *Blues for Mr. Charlie* and LeRoi Jones's *Dutchman*.

"Seasons of Discontent." *The New York Times Book Review* 7 Nov. 1965: 2. On Robert Brustein's *Seasons of Discontent*.

BIBLIOGRAPHY

Uncollected Essays

"Positive Thinking on Pennsylvania Avenue." *Chicago Review* 11 (1957): 21–24. Reprinted in *New Republic* 3 June 1957: 10–11.

"Mrs. Lindberg, Mr. Ciardi, and the Teeth and Claws of the Civilized World." *Chicago Review* 11 (1957): 72–76.

"The Kind of Person I Am." *New Yorker* 29 Nov. 1958: 173–78.

"Recollections from Beyond the Last Rope." *Harper's* July 1959: 42–48.

"Iowa: A Very Far Country Indeed." *Esquire* Dec. 1962: 1932.

"Introduction: Milan Kundera, Edward and God." *American Poetry Review* Mar./Apr. 1974: 5.

"Introduction: Jiri Weil, Two Stories about Nazis and Jews." *American Poetry Review* Sept./Oct. 1974: 22.

"In Search of Kafka and Other Answers." *The New York Times Book Review* 15 Feb. 1976: 6–7.

"Roth and Singer on Bruno Schulz." *The New York Times Book Review* 13 Feb. 1977: 5. Interview with Singer on the publication of *The Street of Crocodiles*.

"The Most Original Book of the Season." *The New York Times Book Review* 30 Nov. 1980: 7. Interview with Milan Kundera on the publication of *The Book of Laughter and Forgetting*.

"A Man Saved by His Skills: An Interview with Primo Levi," *The New York Times Book Review* 12 October 1986: 1.

"A Talk with Aharon Appelfeld," *The New York Times Book Review* 28 February 1988:1.

Interviews

"Jewishness and the Younger Intellectuals." *Commentary* Apr. 1961: 306–59. Symposium

"Second Dialogue in Israel." *Congress Bi-Weekly* 16 Sept. 1963: 4–85. Symposium.

Philip Roth. Interview with Jerre Mangione. National Educational Television, 1966. Prod. Jerome Tookin. (Available from Indiana University Audio-Visual Center.)

"A Visit with Philip Roth." *The New York Times Book Review* 2 Sept. 1979: 1. Interview with James Atlas about *The Ghost Writer*.

"Philip Roth: Should Sane Women Shy Away from Him at Parties." London *Sunday Times Magazine* 22 Mar. 1981: 38–42. Interview with Ronald Hayman about *Zuckerman Unbound*.

"The Ghosts of Roth." *Esquire* Sept. 1981: 92–97. Interview with Alain Finkielkraut.

"What Facts? A Talk with Roth." *The New York Times Book Review* 28 Sept. 1988: 3, 46–47. Interview with Jonathan Brent.

"Philip Roth Faces 'The Facts.'" *Boston Globe* 4 Oct. 1988: Living Sec. 65. Interview with Linda Matchan.

Bibliography

Rodgers, Bernard F., Jr. *Philip Roth: A Bibliography*. 2d ed. Metuchen, NJ: Scarecrow, 1984. Includes primary and secondary works.

Critical Works

Books

Bloom, Harold, ed. *Philip Roth*. New York: Chelsea House, 1986. A useful collection of major essays on Roth, including excerpts from each of the full-length studies on Roth published to date.

Jones, Judith Paterson, and Guinevera A. Nance. *Philip Roth*. New York: Ungar, 1981. Uses Roth's own insights in *Reading Myself and Others* and an interview with him for a psychological/ethical/moral reading of his work. Does not situ-

BIBLIOGRAPHY

ate him in relation to either a Jewish, comic, or American tradition.

Lee, Hermione. *Philip Roth*. New York: Methuen, 1982. Roth's incorporation of a Yiddish-American voice into fiction is the most spectacular of any Jewish American writer. Yet in his response to American experience of the last thirty years he writes out of alienation from both "claustrophobic Jewishness" and "vertiginous Americanness."

McDaniel, John N. *The Fiction of Philip Roth*. Haddonfield, NJ: Haddonfield House, 1974. Roth is a humanist whose concerns are moral and social, and whose artistic vision, though rooted in the particularities of Jewish life, extends outward to embrace the common humanity of all from an essentially secular and skeptical perspective. His protagonists are either activist heroes who self-consciously reject social and domestic norms or victim heroes caught up in the absurdity of the contemporary world.

Meeter, Glenn. *Bernard Malamud and Philip Roth: A Critical Essay*. Grand Rapids, MI: Eerdsmans, 1968. Malamud and Roth as serious writers for whom "Jewish" is an ethnic, sociological, and intellectual term; stern moralists who are yet "romantic" and work to keep a religious spirit alive in a secular world, and whose work invites response in specifically Christian terms.

Milbauer, Asher Z. and Watson, Donald G. *Reading Philip Roth*, New York: St. Martin's Press, 1988. An important collection, including essays by Israeli, English and American critics and fiction-writers, focusing on Roth's achievement as literary artificer.

Pinsker, Sanford. *"The Comedy That Hoits": An Essay on the Fiction of Philip Roth*. Columbia: University of Missouri

BIBLIOGRAPHY

Press, 1975. Roth has written serious fiction meant to attract, not alienate, Jewish readers. His work tries not simply to deal with "hoit," or pain, but to transcend its crippling power. Roth is very talented, but has not yet managed to write a fully satisfying novel.

—, ed. *Critical Essays on Philip Roth*. Boston: Hall, 1982. An invaluable collection. Divided into two parts, it includes both contemporary reviews of the novels and major critical essays on Roth dealing with his controversy with rabbis, community leaders, and critics over the issue of Jewish anti-Semitism, his humor, and his relation to Kafka (see below for a more detailed discussion of some of the articles).

Rodgers, Bernard F., Jr. *Philip Roth*. Boston: Twayne 1978. Roth is an American realist rather than a "Jewish" writer, with ties to James, Dreiser, nineteenth-century American humorists, and contemporary non-Jewish American writers. He constantly experiments with fictional techniques in an effort to come to grips with the moral consequences faced by men and women in contemporary American society.

Articles

Allen, Mary. "Philip Roth: When She Was Good She Was Horrid." *The Necessary Blankness: Women in Major American Fiction of the Sixties*. Urbana: University of Illinois Press, 1976. 70–96. Reprinted in Bloom, *Philip Roth*. Roth's work reveals an obsession with women's power over men. His heroines are the projection of enormous rage and disappointment, yet he is aware of the weaknesses of men, making the interactions of his men and women characters convincing.

Barnes, Julian. "Philip Roth in Israel: *The Counterlife*." *London*

Review of Books, 5 Mar. 1987: 3–9. Roth brilliantly welds "the personal to the public, the hysterical to the historical" through multilayered stories of Jewish American impotence and virility in Israel; assimilation, Zionism, fanaticism, and English anti-Semitism; and the status of story-making and authority in Nathan Zuckerman's fiction.

Charney, Maurice. *Sexual Fiction*. New York: Methuen, 1981. 113–131. *Portnoy's Complaint* is a comic "sexual fiction" that thoroughly sexualizes reality. Freud's essay, "The Most Prevalent Form of Degradation in Erotic Life," is crucial to understanding Alex Portnoy, who is trapped by the guilt of his incestuous love for his mother.

Fiedler, Leslie. "The Image of Newark and the Indignities of Love: Notes on Philip Roth." *Midstream* 5 (1959): 96–99. Reprinted in Pinsker, *Critical Essays*. Lauds Roth as the prose poet laureate, the memorializer of Newark; finds his work is as "vulgar, comical, subtle, pathetic and dirty" as Newark itself, which would have gone unsung without him.

Gross, Barry. "Sophie Portnoy and 'The Opossum's Death': American Sexism and Jewish Anti-Gentilism." *Studies in American Jewish Literature* 3. Ed. Dan Walden. Albany: State University of New York Press, 1983. 166–78. Michael Gold celebrates his mother in his biographical portrait, while Alex Portnoy vilifies his mother; Gold measures his mother by Jewish standards and accepts her strengths, whereas Alex judges by American standards, which are much more gender-rigid and limited.

Howe, Irving. "Philip Roth Reconsidered." *Commentary* Dec. 1972: 69–77. Reprinted in Pinsker, *Critical Essays*. Roth's work since *Goodbye, Columbus* is distorted by personal and ideological self-assertiveness. It derives too much from the tradition of Jewish self-criticism and satire. He is talented, but his creative vision is marred by vulgarity, which undercuts the rich substance of human experience.

Kazin, Alfred. "The Earthly City of the Jews." *The Bright Book of Life*. Boston: Little, Brown, 1973. 144–49. Reprinted in Pinsker, *Critical Essays*. Roth is a second-generation Jewish writer (Bellow and Malamud are first generation, and more celebratory) whose concern is "the self-conscious Jew, newly middle-class" whose identity, though established, is a problem to himself.

Quart, Barbara Koenig. "The Rapacity of One Nearly Buried Alive." *Massachusetts Review* 24 (1983): 590–608. Roth's novels are domestic and personal, concerned with the struggles of American Jewish sons to become men in the face of an "'alien' paternity both psychic and cultural." Their protagonists are caught between the rapacity of the pleasure principle and shame, self-loathing, and sexual guilt.

Schechner, Mark. "Philip Roth." *Partisan Review* 41 (1974): 410–27. Reprinted in Pinsker, *Critical Essays*. One of Roth's most perceptive critics argues that Howe (see above) is insensible to Roth's real gifts: skillful deployment of language, overmastering wit, the exact rendition of subtle psychological truths. His protagonists try to satisfy deep-seated but contrary needs to grow up and to regress, to let go and to hold on, to be both autonomous and dependent.

Solotaroff, Theodore. "Philip Roth: A Personal View." *The Red-Hot Vacuum*. New York: Atheneum, 1970. 306–28. Reprinted in Pinsker, *Critical Essays*. A memoir and appreciation of Roth's early work by a fellow University of Chicago graduate student who sees Roth as writing fresh, gritty fic-

BIBLIOGRAPHY

tion against the cool grain of Flaubert and the modernists Joyce and Mansfield.

Tanner, Tony. "Fictionalized Recall—or 'The Settling of Scores! The Pursuit of Dreams!" *City of Words: American Fiction 1950–1970.* New York: Harper, 1971. 295–321. Roth is a meticulous observer of the social, the familial, and the obsessed self. *Portnoy's Complaint* is an American version of Kafka's *Letter to his Father.* Like Bellow's Herzog, Portnoy is caught between evocations of memory and the desire to purge oneself of those memories and get on with the present.

Whitfield, Stephen J. "Laughter in the Dark: Notes on American-Jewish Humor." *Midstream* Feb. 1978: 48–58. Reprinted in Pinsker, *Critical Essays.* Discusses Roth in the context of the many Jewish humorists in twentieth-century America. The opiate of the Jewish masses, Jewish humor characteristically juxtaposes the lofty and the immediate; exposes absurdity and the disparity between fantasy and actuality; uses irony and ambiguity to reveal the bittersweet quality of life and the limitations of the human condition.

Wirth-Nesher, Hana. "The Artist Tales of Philip Roth." *Prooftexts* 3 (1983): 263–72. Roth's central subject is his own personal drama, the conflict between the Jewish writer bent on freely expressing himself in his art and his moralistic family and readers. His later fiction is both more self-reflexive and more strongly identified with Jewish life.

INDEX

Addams, Jane, 61
Aleichem, Sholem, 56
Allen, Woody, 152
Alliteration, 122–123
"Aloft," 217–220, 222
American heartland, 60, 70
American Jewish life, 21, 23, 35, 39, 41–51, 156–169 *passim*
Anti-Semitism, 34, 80, 161, 163–164, 188, 206, 212, 214, 224–225, 253–254
Arendt, Hannah, 163, 200n.
Assimilation, 35–36, 38, 48–51, 54–58, 83–84, 96 *passim*
Autobiographical fiction, 12, 132–144

Babel, Isaac, 162–163
Bakhtin, Mikhail, 231n.
Barnes, Julian, 231n.
Baseball, 51, 82, 108, 109, 121–131, 228, 240, 253
"Basel" (Switzerland), 207–211, 222–223
Bathroom, 89–90, 92, 94
Bellow, Saul, 17, 39, 81, 86, 162, 243
Berkshires (New England), 156–172
Bildungsroman, 41, 87, 156, 248
Bovary, Madame, 71, 73

Calley, Lieutenant, 103, 105–106
Carnovsky, 172–182, 185, 187, 192, 207
Cervantes *(Don Quixote)*, 19
Chekhov, Anton, 18
Chicago, 60–61, 71, 187
"Christendom," 223–231
Circumcision, 226
Class status, 15, 17, 23–42, 51–53, 61, 75, 94, 165
Columbus, Christopher, 32
Columbus, Ohio, 32, 33
Comic imagination, 19
Community and communal life/values, 21, 50, 54, 63, 92, 155, 164, 171–172, 188, 209, 236
Conrad, Joseph *(Heart of Darkness)*, 127

De Beauvoir, Simone, 84, 102n.
Dickens, Charles, 18, 159
DiMaggio, Joe, 83, 91, 92, 96, 97

Ellison, Ralph, 241
Ethnicity, 12, 17, 31–32, 47, 49–50, 61, 84–86, 96, 237
Everyday life, 17, 39

Family (and family values), 26, 31–34, 39, 41, 48, 66, 82, 92, 132, 136, 155, 237, 239, 248
Fictionalized recall, 12
Fiedler, Leslie, 4
Film (and filmic qualities of Roth's novels), 21–22
Finn, Huckleberry, 18, 45, 123
Fischer, Michael J., 84, 102n.
Flood, Curt, 103, 108–109, 111
Frank, Anne, 168–171, 196, 213

INDEX

Gatsby, Jay *(The Great Gatsby)*, 18, 30
Geertz, Clifford, 232n.
Gender, 17, 84–86, 95–96
Gilbert, Sandra, and Susan Gubar, 201n.
Gilman, Sander, 201n.
"Gloucestershire," 221–231
God, 43–44, 47, 56
Gogol, Nikolai ("The Nose"), 112, 117
Golden, Harry, 241
Goyim (Gentiles), 92, 94, 95, 97
Green, Martin, 244
Gross, Barry, 95, 102n.
Guilt, 77–78, 88, 93, 238

Hasidic Jews, 54
Hemingway, Ernest, 123–124
Herzl, Theodore, 200, 211, 229
Holocaust, the, 54–58, 169, 184, 197, 211, 219, 234, 247

Immigrant world and values (Jewish), 21, 26, 31–32, 36–37, 161
Individualism, 12, 89, 112–113
Innocence, 44, 46, 60
Isaac, Dan, 19n.
Isolation, 45
Isolato, 72
Israel, 169, 204–206, 211–220

James, Henry, 64–65, 159, 162–163
"Jewboy," 86–88, 144, 147, 149, 151–153
Jewishness, 85–87, 97, 163, 185, 213, 218, 226
Jewish American Literature, 18
Jewish Fathers, 146, 156–200, 252
Jewish Mothers, 77–101, 146

Jewish self-hatred, 18, 100, 188, 205, 212, 215, 218
Jewish sons, 67, 75, 77–101, 132–144, 155–172, 174, 227, 239, 252 *passim*
Job (biblical), 18–19, 192
Jones, Judith Paterson, and Guinevera A. Nance, 76n., 154n.
Joyce, James *(Portrait of the Artist as a Young Man)*, 164
"Judea," 211–216, 222–224

Kafka, Franz, 18, 78, 112, 117, 190, 192–193, 200, 233, 238, 242–243
Kazin, Alfred, 85–86, 102n.
Kingston, Maxine Hong, 201n.
Kitchen, the, 35, 89–90, 92, 94
Kundera, Milan, 192, 200, 201n., 233, 242

Lee, Hermione, 232n.
Lelchuk, Alan, 242

Mailer, Norman, 162, 241
Malamud, Bernard, 17, 39, 86, 241
Marginality, 45, 60
Marx Brothers, 19, 152
Masculinity, 15–16, 32, 83–84, 87, 95–97, 100, 112–120, 138–143, 146–147, 166–167, 206, 211
Masturbation, 81, 89–90, 93, 167, 180, 245
Matchan, Linda, 256n.
Melville, Herman *(Moby Dick)*, 18, 80, 122–123, 131, 201n.
Memory, 18, 42, 124
Milbauer, Asher, and Donald Watson, 102n., 201n.
Misogyny, 143
Moi, Toril, 102n.

Names (importance of in Roth's work), 13
Nazis, 166, 194, 197, 211, 242
Neusner, Jacob, 232n.
Newark, 14, 21, 23–26, 36, 40–41, 161, 164, 175, 179, 181, 184, 185, 254

INDEX

New Jersey, 93, 134, 176, 188, 204–205, 211–213, 217, 219, 228, 231, 242–243

New York, 60–61, 66, 94, 185, 205, 212

"Nice Jewish boy," 86–88, 138, 142, 144, 147, 149, 151–153

"1950s," 23, 42, 45, 54, 71, 93, 97, 101, 134, 140–141

Orwell, George, 104

Pale Face, 240
Park, Robert, 61
Pinsker, Sanford, 71, 76n.
Prague (Czechoslovakia), 192–200, 243

Quart, Barbara Koenig, 154n.

Rahv, Philip, 240
Realism (in Roth's work), 17
Redskin, 240
Riesman, David, 10
Richler, Mordecai, 17
Rilke, Rainer Maria, 18, 120, 155, 160, 170, 199–200, 247
Rockwell, Norman, 71
Rodgers, Bernard, 71, 76
Rosenberg, Ethel and Julius, 109
Roth, Philip: career of, 1–7; family, 1–2; overview, 7–18

Major Characters:
Tricky E. Dixon, 10, 103–111, 130
Ozzie Freedman, 42–47, 53, 72, 186, 237
Sheldon Grossbart, 13, 48–51
Libby Herz, 14, 62–70
Paul Herz, 13, 62–70
David Kepesh, 11, 14, 16, 111–120, 144–154, 193, 208, 239, 246–247
Neil Klugman, 10, 13, 14, 15, 21–42, 63

INDEX

E. I. Lonoff, 156–172, 182, 228

Nathan Marx (Sergeant), 48–51

Lucy Nelson, 14, 15, 71–76, 237, 239, 246–247

Brenda Patimkin, 10, 15, 21–42, 63

Eli Peck, 10, 55–58

Alexander Portnoy, 13, 14, 77–101, 123, 134, 138, 142–143, 146–147, 152, 166, 171, 237, 239, 245, 255

Martha Regenhart, 15, 61–70, 246

Word Smith, 122–130

Dr. Spielvogel, 13, 79–80, 90, 98, 100–101, 138, 172, 255

Peter Tarnopol, 16, 132–147, 153, 205–206

Gabe Wallach, 14, 15, 61–70

Henry Zuckerman, 181, 203, 207–218, 221–224, 227–228, 230

Nathan Zuckerman, 13, 14, 16, 132–147, 153, 155–200, 203–231, 248–251

Minor Characters:

Abravanel, 162

Roland Agni, 13, 127, 130

Milton Appel, 185–189

Aunt Gladys, 10, 23, 25–27, 32–33, 39

Helen Baird, 13, 16, 145, 149–153

Roy Bassart, 15, 74, 246–247

Ralph Baumgarten, 150–153

Amy Bellette, 167–171, 182

Rabbi Binder, 43–47, 53, 186

Birgitta, 15, 145, 148–153

Black boy ("Goodbye, Columbus"), 28, 32, 36

Kay Campbell ("The Pumpkin"), 96

Willard Carroll, 71, 74

John F. Charisma, 110

Robert F. Charisma, 106

Dina Dornbusch, 1, 138

Shuki Elchanan, 212–214, 216–217, 229

Epstein, 10
Gil Gamesh, 127–128
Asher, Herz, 69
Dr. Klinger, 13, 114–115, 117–120, 151
Mordecai Lippman, 13, 214, 218, 228
Jimmy Lustig, 13, 219–220, 228
Maria, 204–205, 215, 221–225, 228–229, 251
Sarah Abbott Maulsby ("The Pilgrim"), 96
Susan Seabury McCall, 140
Ronald Nimkin, 98
Claire Ovington, 13, 112, 114–117, 145, 152–153, 247
Julie Patimkin, 24, 28, 30, 33
Mr. Patimkin, 26, 33, 36–37
Ron Patimkin, 26, 30, 31, 36, 39–40
Alvin Pepler, 14, 173–176, 179–180
Mary Jane Reed ("The Monkey"), 97, 99
Arthur Schonbrunn, 116, 145
Sharon Shatsky, 16, 135
Maureen Mezik Johnson Tarnopol, 139–141
Theresa, 15, 67, 70
Leo Tzuref, 55
Uncle Max, 10, 23, 25–27, 33
Mr. Wallach, 66–70
Judge Wapter, 164–166, 168
Carol Zuckerman, 203, 207–208, 210, 215, 222

Collections of Short Fiction:
Goodbye, Columbus, 4, 5, 10, 21–59, 212, 229, 235, 237, 241

Non-Fiction:
The Facts: A Novelist's Autobiography, 19, 248–255
"'I Always Wanted You to Admire My Fasting': or, Looking at Kafka,"
233, 242
"Imagining the Erotic: Three Introductions," 242

"On *The Breast*," 239
"On *The Great American Novel*," 239–240
"On *Portnoy's Complaint*," 238–239
A Philip Roth Reader, 244–248
Reading Myself and Others, 234–243
"Some New Jewish Stereotypes," 241
"Writing About Jews," 241
"Writing American Fiction," 240
"Writing and The Powers that Be," 237–238

Novels:
The Anatomy Lesson, 182–192, 250
The Breast, 111–120, 155, 239, 245, 247
The Counterlife, 202–231, 250–251
The Great American Novel, 6, 120–131, 233, 240
The Ghostwriter, 156–172, 202, 213, 228–229
Letting Go, 3, 5, 15, 61–70, 72, 246
My Life as a Man, 15, 132–145, 153, 202, 205, 209, 253
Our Gang, 103–111, 121, 128, 233, 237
Portnoy's Complaint, 4, 5, 75, 77–101, 144, 145, 172, 199, 225, 229, 237–238
The Professor of Desire, 15, 144–154, 193
When She Was Good, 3, 5, 70–76, 238, 246
Zuckerman Bound, 6, 85, 155–200, 209
Zuckerman Unbound, 172–182

Short Stories:
"The Conversion of the Jews," 42–47, 72, 186
"Defender of the Faith," 48–51, 235
"Eli, The Fanatic," 54–58, 188, 235
"Epstein," 51
"Goodbye, Columbus," 15, 21–42, 62–63
"Novotny's Pain," 246
"On the Air," 6

INDEX

"The Prague Orgy," 192–200
"You Can't Tell a Man by the Song He Sings," 51

Sacco and Vanzetti, 109
Satire (Roth as satirist), 16–17, 41–42, 47, 54, 103–111, 120, 188–189, 235 *passim*
Schechner, Mark, 85, 102n.
Schlemiehl, 162
Sex, 22–24, 28–30, 77, 99–101, 192–200 *passim*
Shakespeare, William, 18, 116–117
Shikses (Gentile women), 17, 95, 97, 136, 138, 142, 239
Singer, Isaac Bashevis, 162
Singer, Israel Joshua, 162, 187
Skvorecky, Josef, 193, 200
Social mobility, 15, 23–32, 36
Solotaroff, Theodore, 76, 77, 102n.
Stereotypes, 16–17, 34, 241
Stewart, Jimmy, 83
Suburbia, 18, 21, 23–42, 58, 64, 236–237
Swift, Jonathan, 18, 103–104

Thomas, D. M., 231n.
Thoreau, Henry David, 71
Transformations, 111–120, 246
Trilling, Diana, 238
Trilling, Lionel (*The Liberal Imagination*), 19

University of Chicago, 61, 65
Urban life, 17–18, 26–42, 54, 160
Uris, Leon, 241

Vietnam War, 103–105, 110, 173
Vocation, artistic, 155–172

INDEX

Wagman, Frederica, 242
Whitman, Walt, 123, 220, 228
Williams, Margaret Martinson, 2, 252
World War II, 12, 24, 49, 54, 185, 235, 253, 254
Women as victims, 73
"Writers from the Other Europe," 233

Yeats, William Butler, 229, 232n.
Yiddish, 17, 55–56, 158, 193, 195, 198, 242

Zionism, 199–200, 204–205, 211–218, 223, 229